Strategies for Sustainability

Latin America

IUCN: The World Conservation Union

Founded in 1948, The World Conservation Union brings together states, government agencies and a diverse range of non-governmental organizations in a unique world partnership. IUCN has over 800 members in all, spread across some 125 countries.

As a Union, IUCN seeks to influence, encourage and assist societies throughout the world to conserve the integrity and diversity of nature and ensure that any use of natural resources is equitable and ecologically sustainable. A central Secretariat coordinates the IUCN programme and serves the Union membership, representing their views on the world stage and providing them with the strategies, services, scientific knowledge and technical support they need to achieve their goals. Through its six commissions, IUCN draws together over 6000 expert volunteers in project teams and action groups, focusing in particular on species and biodiversity conservation and management of habitats and natural resources. The Union has helped many countries prepare National Conservation Strategies and demonstrates the application of its knowledge through the field projects it supervises. Operations are increasingly decentralized and are carried forward by an expanding network of regional and national offices, located principally in developing countries.

IUCN builds on the strength of its members, networks and partners to enhance their capacity and support global alliances to safeguard natural resources at local, regional and international levels.

The Strategies for Sustainability Programme of IUCN

Based on the principles of the World Conservation Strategy and *Caring for the Earth* [1], IUCN supports the preparation and implementation of strategies for sustainability in response to requests from governments, communities and NGOs. The Strategies for Sustainability Programme of the IUCN Secretariat and the Working Group on Strategies of the IUCN Commission on Environmental Strategy and Planning (CESP) assist those involved in strategies through a programme aimed at:

- undertaking conceptual development and exchange and analysis of experience concerning strategies throughout the world;
- carrying out demonstration and testing of key elements, tools and methodologies in strategies;
- building regional networks of strategy practitioners; and
- strengthening local capacity by engaging the networks in conceptual development, exchange and analysis of experience, and demonstration activities.

The programme draws on experience with all types of strategies regardless of their sources of support. Working group members include practitioners in national conservation strategies (NCSs), national environmental action plans (NEAPs), Biodiversity Action Plans, Forestry Action Plans (FAPs), and a wide range of provincial (state) and local strategies.

1. IUCN, UNEP and WWF (1991). *Caring for the Earth: A Strategy for Sustainable Living.*
   Earthscan Publications, London.

Strategies for Sustainability

Latin America

Arturo Lopez Ornat, Editor

Strategies for Sustainability Programme

IUCN
The World Conservation Union

EARTHSCAN
Earthscan Publications Ltd., London

Strategies for Sustainability: Latin America was made possible by the generous support of the Swedish International Development Authority, the International Development Resource Centre (IDRC) and the Swiss Agency for Development Cooperation (SDC)

First published in the UK in 1997 by:
Earthscan Publications Limited, in association with IUCN

A catalogue record for this book is available from the British Library

ISBN: 1 85383 272 3

Design: Patricia Halladay

Earthscan Publications Limited, 120 Pentonville Road, London, N1 9JN, UK
Tel: 0171 278 0433   Fax: 0171 278 1142
Email: earthinfo@earthscan.co.uk
Web Site: http://www.earthscan.co.uk

IUCN Publications Services Unit, 219c Huntingdon Road, Cambridge, CB3 0DL, UK
IUCN Communications Division, Rue Mauverney 28, CH-1196 Gland, Switzerland

The views of the authors expressed in this book, and the presentation of the material, do not imply the expression of any opinion whatsoever on the part of IUCN concerning the legal status of any country, territory or area of its authorities, or concerning the delimitation of its frontiers or boundaries. IUCN disclaims any errors or omissions in the translation from the original Spanish.

Printed and bound in the UK by Biddles Ltd, Guildford and King's Lynn

Printed on acid and elemental chlorine free paper, sourced from sustainably managed forests and processed according to an environmentally responsible manufacturing system.

Contents

PART 2: CASE STUDIES

CENTRAL AMERICA

Costa Rica: Strategy for Sustainable Development

Nicaragua: National Conservation Strategy

Kuna-Yala, Panama: Sustainability for Comprehensive Development

Majé-Bayano, Panama: Sustainable Development Strategy

Petén Region, Guatemala: Sustainable Development Strategy

Preface

This publication is part of an IUCN series of Regional Reviews of Strategies for Sustainability covering Asia, Africa and Latin America. The series is devoted to an analysis of lessons learned in multi-sectoral strategies at national, provincial and local levels. It is a joint effort by the Strategies for Sustainability Programme of the World Conservation Union (IUCN) and its Commission on Environmental Strategy and Planning (CESP). It was carried out in cooperation with other organizations such as the World Bank, The United Nations Development Programme (UNDP), The International Institute for Environment and Development (IIED) and The World Resources Institute (WRI) to assemble and analyze experience with strategies, and use this information to improve future strategy development and implementation.

Each volume consists of a status report that summarizes the status of strategies in the region, a synthesis of case studies, and individual case studies of selected strategies. The review attempts to cover only a sample of the region's strategies, recognizing that reviews such as this can never capture all the experiences that a region has to offer. The information presented here is up to date at the time the case studies were compiled (July 1993 – March 1995).

The case studies are not intended to be evaluations. They are analytical histories of strategies, providing a summary of basic information and lessons learned that has not before been readily available.

The case studies were prepared by members of the IUCN/CESP Working Group of Strategies for Sustainability and staff of the IUCN regional and national offices, including individuals who have been closely involved in the development and implementation of the strategies, and who are from the country concerned. The team includes the participants and resource teams from the 1993 Isla Taboga Workshop and the 1995 Petén Workshop.

It is important to emphasize that much of the field work undertaken in these cases are pioneering efforts in strategic planning and implementation. The educational value of the workshops was increased by participants' willingness to discuss their experiences frankly and openly. They focused on problems they encountered and lessons they had learned; and they considered their failures as good learning opportunities. Because of their openness and ability to reflect on their experience, the learning value of the workshops and case studies was increased significantly.

This text was originally written in Spanish by Arturo López Ornat; however IUCN felt it was important to translate the case studies into English, so that the experience of developing and implementing strategies, particularly at the local level in Latin America, could be shared with other regions in the world. With any translation from an original language, there are bound to be phrases that may not be familiar to readers of English. We hope that this will not prove too much of an inconvenience to readers.

We hope these experiences provide valuable information, stimulation and motivation to others facing similar challenges elsewhere. The views presented in the case studies do not necessarily reflect those of the government agencies or the officials involved.

Acknowledgements

IUCN wishes to thank the authors of the case studies and the workshop participants for giving so freely of their time and experience in order to share with others the lessons they have learned through perseverance, trial and error. We are particularly grateful to Arturo López Ornat for his long hours of work in coordinating the work of the individual case studies and for compiling this volume. Peter Whiting ably undertook the task of translating the text into English.

We are also grateful for the financial support that enabled us to organize and host the two workshops at which these case studies were discussed and analyzed, and finally, for the funds to publish and distribute this volume.

Local arrangements for the Isla Taboga workshop were made by IUCN–ORMA's Panama Office, and for the Petén workshop by the SEGEPLAN Office in Petén and by IUCN–ORMA. Funds for the Taboga workshop were provided by the International Development Research Centre (IDRC), the Swedish Development Authority (SIDA) and by the United Nations Development Programme (UNDP). Funds for the Petén workshop were provided by IDRC. Funds for the publication of this volume were provided by the Swiss Agency for Development Cooperation (SDC). To these organizations, we offer our thanks for their support.

Nancy MacPherson
Coordinator
Strategies for Sustainability Programme
IUCN HQ, Gland Switzerland

Workshop and Case Study Participants

Isla Taboga, Panama Workshop, 1993

The participants at the Isla Taboga workshop were: Jorge Albán Gomez (Ecuador), Ricardo Almanza (Panama), Augusto Angel Maya (Ecuador), Dionisio Batista (Panama), Miguel Canals (Puerto Rico), Victor Cedeño (Nicaragua), Avecita Chicchón (Peru), Otoniel Gonzalez (Panama), Carlos Hernandez (Guatemala), Oscar Lücke (Costa Rica), Odilia Maessen (Canada), Juan Mayr (Colombia), Carmen Miranda (Bolivia), Rolando Mendoza (Costa Rica), Victor Merino (Peru), Nydia E Morales (Panama), Carlos de Paco (Costa Rica), Marco Antonio Palacios (Guatemala), Rosadela Pinzón (Panama), Omar Ramirez Tejada (Dominican Republic), Eric Rodriguez (Panama), Guillermo Rodriguez (Colombia), Luis A Rojas (Costa Rica), Pedro Rosabal (Cuba), Sebastião Salles de Sá (Brazil), Maria Virginia Sandino (Nicaragua), Eduardo Soares (Brazil), Gustavo Suarez de Freitas (Peru) and Maryi Valderrama (Colombia). The sessions were moderated by: Alejandro Imbach, Oscar Lücke, Nancy MacPherson, Juan Mayr, Marco A Palacios, Rosadela Pinzón, Robert Prescott-Allen and Pedro Rosabal. The organizing team and secretariat were made up by: Marcella Bonilla (Colombia), Luis Castello (Argentina), Alejandro Imbach (Argentina), Arturo López Ornat (Spain), Nancy MacPherson (Canada), Robert Prescott-Allen (Canada), Alberto Salas Ávila (Costa Rica) and Vivienne Solís (Costa Rica).

Petén, Guatemala Workshop, 1995

The participants at the Petén workshop were: Jorge Albán Gomez (Ecuador), Augusto Angel Maya (Ecuador), César Barrientos (Guatemala), Dionisio Batista (Panama), Allen Cordero (Guatemala), Eric Dudley (UK), Juan Carlos Godoy (Guatemala), Otoniel Gonzalez (Panama), José Guillermo Gonzalez Marcos (Guatemala), Carlos Hernandez (Guatemala), Enrique Lahmann (Costa Rica), Alain Meyrat (Nicaragua), Carlos Raul Montes (Guatemala), Natalia Ortiz (Colombia), Marco Antonio Palacios (Guatemala), Omar Ramirez Tejada (Dominican Republic), Ana Victoria Rodriguez (Guatemala), Guillermo Rodriguez (Colombia), Luis A Rojas (Costa Rica), Hernando Sanchez (Colombia), Tomi Tuomasjukka (Finland), Florangel Villegas (Venezuela) and Néstor Windevoxhel Lora (Venezuela). The sessions were moderated by: Jorge Albán (Ecuador), César Barrientos (Guatemala), Alejandro Imbach (Argentina), Natalia Ortiz (Colombia), Marco A Palacios (Guatemala), Guiselle Rodriguez (Costa Rica) and Alberto Salas (Costa Rica). The organizing team and secretariat were made up by: Alejandro Imbach (Argentina), Arturo López Ornat (Spain), Alberto Salas Ávila (Costa Rica), Florangel Villegas (Venezuela) and Néstor Windevoxhel (Venezuela).

Part 1:
Introduction

1 Introduction

This volume, which has been translated from the original Spanish text, contains an analysis of 15 selected strategies for sustainability in Latin America, their common themes and a summary of the lessons learned. The original Spanish text contains an annexe of summary charts of an additional nine strategies and projects which were not developed into full case studies. These charts are not available in the English translation.

2 What are Sustainable Development Strategies?

Sustainable development strategies are participatory and cyclical processes of planning and action to achieve three objectives – economic, ecological and social – in a balanced and integrated way. There is a wide range of strategies at international, national, provincial/state and local levels, including conservation strategies, environmental action plans, and sustainable development strategies. Sustainable development strategies aim to achieve all three objectives; other strategies emphasize one or two of them.

Strategies may be multi-sectoral, embracing a wide range of sectors, interests and issues. Or they may be thematic, focusing on particular sectors or topics like biodiversity, education, climate change, energy, health or population. There are other types of strategies which focus on only one or two of these objectives. Strategies may be comprehensive, covering a broad spectrum of sectors; or targeted, focusing on the sustainability of a particular sector, such as forestry, conservation, fisheries or education.

Since 1980, more than 75 countries have initiated multi-sector strategies at national, provincial, state and local levels. Considerable experience in undertaking strategies has been gained, but it has not been systematically organized or analyzed until recently.

Strategies are *processes*, not documents. The strategy documents are merely instruments to make a strategy explicit, so that it may be discussed, agreed and applied by a broad spectrum of participants.

Strategies are necessary for resolving complex problems involving many actors. A strategy is not a plan, although planning is an important part of a strategy. A plan is linear, rigid and frequently sectoral. A strategy is a dynamic process dealing with a diversity of groups and interests. Strategies are participatory and adaptive, taking advantage of and strengthening existing capacities and generating inter-sectoral links. Strategies reassess the situation periodically through a system of monitoring and assessment, and they adapt accordingly.

3 Types of Strategies in Latin America

A sample of strategies taking place in Latin America appears in Table 1. They include international, national, regional and local strategies. Of the 25 examples listed, 15 case studies have been developed more fully in this volume. Summaries of the remaining examples are contained in the Spanish volume.

In our opinion, a sustainable development strategy includes the areas of economic development, social development and environmental and conservational development in its analysis and policy formulation.

The same objectives are considered in FAPs. In 1988, the World Bank made FAPs a condition of granting credit as an attempt to slow deforestation and to promote sustainable use of tropical forests through forest management programmes, agroforestry, soil and biodiversity conservation, organization and industrial development. FAPs may be joint projects and may include components aimed at strengthening and developing national institutions and non-governmental organizations (NGOs). They also include measures to strengthen the policies and the legal and institutional frameworks of the countries concerned. FAPs may therefore be considered strategies, but with a sectoral approach (forestry).

The biosphere reserves status proposed in 1976 by the United Nations Educational, Scientific and Cultural Organization (UNESCO) aims to create a world network of protected natural areas, where representative samples of the ecosystems and species they contain are preserved, where traditional cultures found within are strengthened, and where new technologies are tested or adapted with the participation of the local population. Some biosphere reserves now have over ten years of experience in trying to combine these different objectives, and provide an excellent source of experience and learning.

4 Selecting and Classifying Cases

The selection of cases analyzed in this regional review (Table 1) was based on the following criteria:

- the approach was inter-sectoral with sustainable development objectives;
- participatory planning was applied;
- an inter-sectoral action plan was drawn up with broad participation and distribution of responsibilities;
- policies were formulated in a consensus document, and officially adopted;
- actions have already been initiated to apply the strategy; and
- the planning/action process has been underway for a number of years and there is a body of existing methodological experience.

Not all the cases listed in Table 1 comply completely with all the criteria given above. There are differences of approach, scale and implementation time. Some cases are clearly sustainable development strategies, with several years of experience; others offer a potential strategic approach to a variety of actions lacking a cohesive framework. A number of 'projects', for instance, are in fact working towards an alternative to 'unsustainable' development, but without a strategic framework. The geographical scale of the strategies also differs greatly, from 5,000 hectares in Puerto Rico to over a million in Petén or Amazonia.

The objectives of social and economic development and an improved quality of life are implicit in all the cases analyzed, and explicit in the sustainable development cases ('SD' in Table 1). The other cases have a sectoral focus, concentrating mainly on conservation and/or the management of natural resources. The conservation of biodiversity, sustainable forest management and environmental education are the sectors which have received most attention. A focus on macroeconomic and financial aspects of sustainable development is missing in many of the cases, except in those in Cuba, Costa Rica, Ecuador and Nicaragua.

The selected cases differ in terms of their main themes, and they embrace a broad spectrum of geographical, political and organizational factors, and varying degrees of success in achieving objectives. A comparative analysis is given of the key factors in the success and the failure of these processes.

5 Status of Strategies

The status of these cases is summarized in Table 1, with an indication of their formal link with the development plans of the countries or regions concerned. While these strategies represent the most advanced experience in the region, definitive results are still to be seen.

These are all pioneering processes; approximately half of the strategies analyzed are still at the formulation stage. The others have reached the proposal document stage. The Sierra Maestra Strategy in Cuba is well into implementation.

A document does not necessarily guarantee action or a change in development policies. In five cases (APTA, Guánica, Héroes y Mártires, Sierra Nevada and Tambopata), practical action has been taken in specific sectors and results have been produced in the field without any document.

Table 1   Status of cases analysed (1995)

Strategy	Country	Approach	Status (implementation) (document)							Integration in development plans				
			A B C D E F G							TT	PC	PS	AG	NO
International														
Gulf of Fonseca*	Salvador, Honduras, Nicaragua	C/D	D								•			
National														
Cuba*		C/D	A							•				
Costa Rica		SD	B, D								•	•		
Nicaragua		SD	E								•			
Peru*		C/D	B, E											•
Regional														
Amazonia	Ecuador	SD	F									•		
Bocas del Toro*	Panama	SD	C, D								•	•	•	
Petén	Guatemala	SD	A								•		•	
San Martin*	Peru	C+ET	E										•	•
Sierra Nevada	Colombia	SD	C, F								•		•	
Tortuguero	Costa Rica	SD	B, D								•	•	•	
Local														
El Beni*	Bolivia	C/D	B, F								•		•	
Guánica	Puerto Rico	SD	B, G								•	•		
Heroes y Martires	Nicaragua	AF	B, G								•			
Majé-Bayano	Panama	C+FO	B, G								•	•	•	
Mata Atlantica	Brazil	C/D	B, G								•		•	
Samaná	Dominican Rep.	C/D	C, E								•	•		
Sierra Maestra	Cuba	SD	A							•				
Tambopata-Candamo	Peru	SD	B, G								•		•	
Projects														
APTA*	Brazil	AF	C, G								•		•	
Cinturón Verde*	Guatemala	Urban	B, G								•	•		
Kuna-Yala	Panama	C+FO	C, G								•	•	•	
Quintana Roo*	Mexico	C+FO	A							•				
Pikín-Guerrero*	Nicaragua	AF	B								•		•	
Talamanca	Costa Rica	SD	C, G								•	•		

See Box 1 for explanation of symbols

* Detailed case studies not available in this volume; summaries appear in the Spanish volume

Box 1: Symbols used in Table 1

Approach

SD	Sustainable Development
C/D	C + Development element
AF	Agroforestry
C	Conservation/Environment
ET	Education/Training
FO	Forest and/or Water

Status

A	Official implementation, binding for all government sectors
B	Applied by some governmental or non-governmental participants
C	Applied by non-governmental sectors
D	Document agreed by participants but not adopted by the government
E	Document formulated, but not agreed by all participant sectors
F	Document in course of preparation
G	Document preparation not yet initiated

Integration in Development Plans

TT	Strategy totally integrated within government development plans
PC	Strategy partially integrated (includes sectoral plans)
PS	Strategy has political support and document is awaiting official adoption
AG	Specific agreements have been signed for its partial implementation
NO	Strategy either not integrated formally, or outside development planning

National Strategies: Summary

The National Strategies of Costa Rica (ECODES) and Nicaragua cover a broad spectrum of environmental, social and economic objectives, and may therefore be considered sustainable development strategies. Those of Cuba and Peru are aimed basically at the conservation of natural resources, although they also take into account elements of socio-economic development when these are related to conservation issues.

1 Origin and Present Situation

In all these cases the initiative started with the natural resources sectors of government. In Costa Rica and Peru, national and international NGOs played a fundamental role in promoting the idea in government departments. In Nicaragua, the process was stimulated by international cooperation. In Cuba, it emerged from successful experiments in several buffer zones, particularly in the Sierra Maestra.

Although there was a consensus among participants in these strategies on the actions required, only in the case of Cuba was the document officially adopted by government. ('A' status in Table 1). In Cuba, 22 government bodies are taking

part in the implementation process, although the strategy is limited geographically to the National System of Protected Areas, which covers 12 per cent of the island's area.

In Peru, the strategy is stalled due to political instability and the dissolution of the government agencies (Planning and Natural Resources) which initiated its formulation in 1989. In Costa Rica, the process was halted during the legislative period (1990–94) when the ruling party was replaced. Partly as a result of this, the strategy was formulated by technicians and experts who were selected on a personal basis; even though some of them were officials, they did not officially represent their institutions. Costa Rica's strategy is being reactivated by the present government (1994–98), whose Declaration for Sustainable Development, accompanied by a programme of concrete measures, constitutes the official policy of the present legislature.

2 Development of Processes

All national strategies have emerged from an inter-sectoral analysis of conservation and development problems, drawing on the expertise of professionals from different disciplines. The methods used have included sectoral working groups, plenary workshops, public consultations, and the circulation and revision of draft proposal documents. The business and financial sectors did not take part in formulating the proposals in the cases of Costa Rica and Peru.

In those two cases in particular, there was a tendency to emphasize the production of a document as the main result, with the development of the process and the implementation of actions left to a second stage. There is a consensus among strategy experts that, in order to keep the process alive, responsibilities have to be shared through implementation of practical activities throughout the process, with the support of a coordinating team or secretariat. The absence of both these conditions in the cases of Costa Rica and Peru also explains why the strategies were not implemented. Until 1994, the action taken in both of these cases was initiated by NGOs and/or individual professionals.

In Cuba and Nicaragua, many ministries and government departments are involved in formulating, approving and applying the strategies, including regional and municipal governments (all the municipalities of Nicaragua are involved in the Cuban Protected Areas scheme). Except in the case of Cuba, all the strategies depended on external funding during their formulation.

3 Main Results

The implementation of sustainable development strategies has been limited mainly by structural problems and external factors: in Costa Rica and Peru by heavy external debt and the socio-environmental problems generated by structural adjustment programmes; in Cuba by the difficult economic situation created by the socio-economic sanctions imposed on the country; and in Nicaragua both by economic difficulties and the political and social consequences of the recent war.

Although these national strategies are still in their early stages, they have all produced some very positive results:

- the strategies of Costa Rica, Cuba and Peru were included in the presentations of those countries given at the UN Conference on Environment and Development (UNCED, Rio de Janeiro, 1992); Cuba's strategy is also part of the Cuban Government's commitments for Agenda 21 and the Convention on Biological Diversity;
- government planning for the strategies included the participation of NGOs in Peru, Costa Rica and Nicaragua;
- inter-sectoral coordination structures were set up in Nicaragua and Cuba as part of the formulation processes;

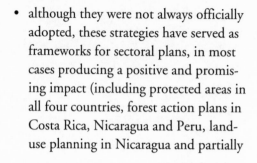

- although they were not always officially adopted, these strategies have served as frameworks for sectoral plans, in most cases producing a positive and promising impact (including protected areas in all four countries, forest action plans in Costa Rica, Nicaragua and Peru, land-use planning in Nicaragua and partially in Cuba, environmental education in Costa Rica and Cuba); and
- in Costa Rica and Peru national strategies contributed indirectly to the start of local strategies in La Amistad, Tortuguero, Inka, Grau, Loreto and Mariátegui.

Sub-national Strategies: Summary and Analysis

1 Origin of Initiatives

The initiatives have originated both in the government sector (especially in Central America and Cuba) and with NGOs (in South America). Conceptually, they could be said to be derived from the contribution made by the World Conservation Strategy (WCS, 1980), UNESCO's Man and Biosphere Programme (MAB) and the development of FAPs.

Economic crisis and large-scale environmental problems were the most common triggering factors, confirming the human tendency to react to problems rather than anticipate them. The problems are substantial and originate from deforestation and the socio-economic failure of inappropriate development initiatives in the American tropics in previous decades.

The conservation of biodiversity provided the main stimulus in many of the sub-national cases. The sponsors were either NGOs or national park services with the objectives of preserving extremely fragile and valuable areas. In many cases, socio-economic objectives were subsequently added to conservation goals, in response to the lack of interest or even opposition shown by local communities towards purely conservation objectives (El Beni, Tambopata, Tortuguero); or else as a reaction to the pressure exerted by communities to obtain development alternatives in the neighbourhood of protected natural areas (Amazonia, Mata Atlántica, Talamanca). In fact, many of the selected local cases are being developed around protected natural areas of international significance; some have been classified by UNESCO as biosphere reserves.

The concerns of the target population acted as a stimulus in the cases of APTA, Kuna-Yala, Quintana Roo and Talamanca (and partially in Tambopata).

The formulation of FAPs created an interest in planning in the case of Kuna-Yala, but in general a reverse effect has been produced, insofar as the introduction of sustainable development strategies has stimulated the development of the forestry sector through the implementation of FAPs, as in the cases of ECODES and Tortuguero in Costa Rica, and in Bocas del Toro and Majé-Bayano in Panama.

A common problem provided a sufficient impulse and rallying point for initiating or strengthening some of the strategies, bringing together very different and even traditionally opposed sectors. For example, in Sierra Nevada (Colombia), interests as diverse as those of indige-nous peoples, major land-owners, guerrilla fighters, drug traffickers and landless peasants all converged on the need to pre-serve water and to regulate water supplies in the Sierra. The serious socio-environmental impact of the spread of the monoculture banana cultivation united all the sectors in favour of a strategy for the Tortuguero plains in Costa Rica, while in the Caribbean, the cases of Guánica and Samaná were initiated by the local authorities and NGOs as a response to the prospect of unregulated tourism.

2 Common Aspects

All the sub-national strategies and practically all the projects are situated in areas with high biological diversity value, and are subject to strict ecological constraints on intensive agricultural production. Some of the cases are faced with the typical situation of a tropical agricultural frontier, while four (Guánica, Samaná, Sierra Maestra and Sierra Nevada) are in areas of colonization, more stable but also recent. Only APTA and Pikín-Guerrero are located in traditional agricultural areas, and only one project is located in an urban periphery, namely the 'Cinturón Verde' (green belt) in Guatemala.

All these areas are socially and economically marginalized as a consequence of underdevelopment. They share similar development difficulties and have in common ecological problems derived from deforestation, structural problems such as lack of land tenure, limited institutional structure, and poor or nonexistent public services. They also suffer from drawbacks such as immigration and colonization by cultures which are not adapted to the environment, population growth, a low educational level, and poor or nonexistent organizational structures. Other common features include lack of credit services, technical support or alternatives to the system of monoculture, extensive cattle farming, forest 'mining' and other forms of non-sustainable extractive production. The most critical strategies are those involving multiple resource-use conflicts and structural problems, thus requiring an innovative and consistent management regime.

3 Integrating Strategies in Development Planning

Although the Latin American strategies have only been integrated to a limited extent in national and/or sub-national development planning systems, all have exerted a direct or indirect influence on sectoral planning, particularly in the areas of conservation and forest management.

Official approval

The documents prepared for three strategies (Mata Atlántica, Sierra Maestra and Petén) ('A' status in Table 1) have now been officially approved. Most of the remainder have been internally approved by the organizations which took part in their preparation, but have not been made official by the government.

Multi-sector Participation

The most exceptional case is that of Sierra Maestra in Cuba, which has been approved by law. It is managed by an intersectoral governing board on which six ministries are represented, and which is answerable to the Council of Ministers. The cases of Petén and Bocas del Toro are also noteworthy insofar as the strategies were prepared under the authority of the countries' planning ministries. The strategy for Majé (Panama), although still in preparation, also depends on an interministerial committee. In all the other cases, the only ministry officially involved has been that of natural resources or a local equivalent, and only six cases have involved local authorities (Amazonia, Guánica, Sierra Nevada) or regional governments (Mata Atlántica, Petén and San Martín).

As a result of the limited degree of integration, the strategies tend to be looked upon as additions to rather than integral elements of the planning process. They are generally considered to be chiefly focused on environmental activities, although some have been included as part of the national park services (El Beni, Guánica, Samaná, Tambopata).

Direct and Indirect Results

The strategies had a very positive impact by introducing an environmental component, or a concern for such a component, to the development planning of all these areas. In some cases, there were no development plans for the areas concerned (El Beni, Samaná, Sierra Nevada, Tambopata and Tortuguero); in others the local administrative authorities directly involved in the main aspects of development were weak. For instance, in Bocas del Toro (Panama), the strategy took precedence over formal planning, introducing a preventive or anticipatory environmental component in a region which was still relatively undisturbed. A similar effect may be produced by strategies which are in the development phase for Amazonia (Ecuador), El Beni (Bolivia), Majé (Panama), Samaná (Dominican Republic) and San Martín (Peru).

In almost all the cases, official approval of the strategies is still pending. This does not, however, imply that no official action is being taken or that benefits are not felt in the system.

- Most of the strategies have had favourable effects on the planning of protected natural areas (in practically all cases), the forest sector (in Quintana

Roo since 1984 and in the three Panamanian cases since 1988) with the implementation of Forest Action Plans, water regulation (Pikín-Guerrero, Majé, Sierra Maestra, Sierra Nevada), formal education (San Martín, Pikín-Guerrero, Tortuguero); and

- Some of the projects which have had a greater impact in the field (APTA in Brazil, Quintana Roo forest plan, Comarca Kuna-Yala in Panama) have been organized and developed without the assistance of state institutions. These cases have been purposefully kept outside the framework of the institutions, partly because of the weakness or non-existence of an institutional framework, or because of excessive bureaucracy. Generally speaking, those involved deplore the overlapping interests and the lack of coordination between institutions, the frequent changes of priorities in institu-tional programmes, and the lack of any 'institutional memory', which forces the reiteration of the same requests.

4   Formulating the Strategy

Information Analysis

One of the first steps in a strategy for sustainability should be an inter-sectoral analysis which takes account of multi-sectoral structural development problems. This was done in some of the cases (Amazonia, Bocas del Toro, Sierra

Maestra, Petén, Tambopata, Tortuguero). In all the other cases, either the analysis was limited to specific sectors, or major sectors were omitted from the analysis altogether.

For instance, an analysis of existing **institutional and organizational capacity** is essential to ensure that efforts are optimized and to encourage participation in concrete action. For each institution or organization involved in the strategy, the facts to be assessed include its mandate and its role, its capacities, strengths, weaknesses, financial and human re-sources. This type of analysis was completed in the cases of Guánica, Majé, Mata Atlántica, Petén, Samaná, Sierra Nevada, Sierra Maestra, Talamanca and Tortuguero. The **macro-economic and financial situation** of each region is also frequently overlooked, as is the analysis of loopholes and opportunities in current **laws and regulations** which might affect sustainable development.

Drafting the Document

The formulation of documents was mentioned in all cases as a tool of analysis, common reflection and a focus for the generation of ideas. The sub-national strategies have been less likely than national strategies to put emphasis on the production of documents as the main achievement of the technical teams, although this has been the case with El

Beni, Bocas del Toro and Samaná, and to some extent in Tortuguero. This has had the effect of diminishing the priority of field actions and hence the momentum and interest of participants in the process.

The documents, which frequently contain collated summaries of the socio-environmental data for each region, propose general sectoral guidelines. Four strategies (Mata Atlántica, Petén, Sierra Maestra and Tortuguero) established measurable objectives, criteria, procedures and action priorities individually for each sector.

5   Content of proposals

Land-use Planning

Most of the plans to emerge from these strategies have concerned either land-use planning or the conservation of biological diversity in all regional and local strategies; forest management (in all cases except Samaná and Sierra Nevada); and education in Guánica, Petén, San Martín, Sierra Maestra, Sierra Nevada and Tortuguero.

Land-use planning is a basic tool for building a model of sustainable development in rural areas. It facilitates inter-sectoral integration, the environmentally appropriate location of productive activities, the resolution of land tenure problems and the establishment of ecological, socio-economic and cultural criteria for external assistance.

Future Scenarios

Scenarios were prepared in three cases: Petén, Sierra Maestra and Tortuguero. Scenarios are important for strategic planning, and are useful in generating interest among policy-makers. All three strategies have drawn up population projections, amongst others, which depict alarming scenarios. They propose controlling the load capacity of ecosystems by diversifying economic activities, raising productivity and establishing a minimum size for single-family farms. It is difficult to predict the impact of these measures, since the areas concerned are suffering the consequences of immigration and non-sustainable development from neighbouring regions. According to the scenario, while strategies may be successful in raising the quality of life of local inhabitants, they will also attract more immigration. This is a major concern for all the technical teams and advisers involved in strategies located in buffer zones and agricultural frontier areas.

6   Internalizing Strategies: Participation

Internalization

Strategies must be internalized if they are to have a significant influence over development. While the strategies themselves have to be sustainable, they have to be based on and take advantage of both local and national opportunities, capacities, resources and initiatives. Participation is the tool which will most likely ensure that a strategy is internalized and well adapted to local conditions. This implies understanding local needs and assuming shared responsibility for action.

The importance of participation to the strategic process has been recognized by all working teams, although some feel that they have not placed enough emphasis on it. Where strategies have produced a document, it has been achieved by technical teams in consultation with those directly concerned. In general, technical teams have not placed the same emphasis on participation and on shared responsibility with the target communities and groups. The cases of Sierra Maestra, Sierra Nevada, Tambopata and Tortuguero are exceptional in this respect. All the projects, however, (APTA, Cinturón Verde, Kuna-Yala, Quintana Roo, Pikín-Guerrero and Talamanca) are broadly participatory in design.

Internalizing the strategies means offering appropriate alternatives, incentives and guidelines which are acceptable to the greatest possible majority. Strategies must

be made attractive to governments and understandable by all sectors. They can focus initially on the less contentious problems and facilitate the government's task by explaining the practical benefits to be derived in both the short- and long-term, by proposing possible improvements in all sectors, and by providing a series of tools and actions to ensure that the strategies do not remain mere planning exercises.

One of the lessons learned in this respect is that achieving real participation depends on using common concepts and simple language. In some cases, it was pointed out that terms such as 'reserve' and 'strategy' are inappropriate since they may be interpreted by local populations as referring to plans which are either restrictive or open to preconceptions by people outside the communities. Some use the term 'multiple-use zone' instead of 'buffer zone', or 'agreement' instead of 'strategy'.

It is advisable to reduce the set of issues to one or two common problems and try to resolve them. In Guánica, Samaná, Sierra Maestra, Sierra Nevada, Tambopata and Tortuguero, for instance, it was found that solving a single problem in a community at the beginning of the process was an effective way of achieving credibility and gaining the trust of the local population.

Participation During the Formulation of the Document

One way of creating a feeling of shared responsibility is to encourage participation in the preparation of the initial proposal which is submitted to sponsors and donors. In the cases of Guánica and Quintana Roo, recipient groups participated in this stage of the process. Another possibility is sharing the process of obtaining information in the field in such a way that each participant contributes some of the information. This approach, which establishes strong bonds from the outset, was very helpful for internalizing strategies in the cases of APTA, Guánica, Kuna-Yala, Petén, Tambopata and Tortuguero. Once the draft documents had been produced, however, they were discussed among the technicians but not always circulated among the full constituency. Only in the cases of Guánica, Petén, Sierra Maestra and Tortuguero were strategy objectives and priorities arrived at by agreement with those concerned.

Frequently the teams of specialists chose to share their thoughts and conclusions with others concerned, either at meetings or workshops. Analysis tends to show, however, that consultations held after the proposals are formulated do not have the same internalizing and binding effect as full participation in the preparation of proposals.

Internal Conflicts and External Enemies

One problem which all the processes have in common is internal conflicts among participants. These conflicts are often due to rivalries either between government organizations or between NGOs. When the process is opened up to different sectors, which perhaps have never before tried to resolve common problems together, latent conflicts tend to surface. However this also provides an opportunity to resolve such conflicts early in the process, as was the case in Amazonas, El Beni, Guánica, Majé, Sierra Nevada, Tambopata and Tortuguero. Participation may generate short-term conflicts, but these are likely to be of less magnitude than those it helps to avoid in the longer term.

Half the cases mention outside interests which were openly opposed to the strategy and which brought pressure to bear in order to stop the processes. These included timber and mining companies, multinationals, land speculators and political and economic sectors benefiting from anarchic conditions. Some cases were able to overcome this resistance and are contiuing to do so in different ways, either by having the strategies officially adopted, or else by bringing into the process those interests which have generally been left out. Although most of these sectors are traditionally more interested in short-term economic returns, the forestry, tourism and fishing sectors have recently shown that they could overcome their initial reluctance (for reasons including stock depletion, availability of markets, credit and tax benefits, or simply environmental awareness) and take advantage of multi-sectoral alliances for sustainable production.

7 Prospects for Continuity

Almost all the strategies analyzed claim some political support at government and/or ministerial level. This support is particularly useful where institutional capacity is weak and where there is little cooperation between institutions. It can facilitate inter-departmental cooperation, break down institutional barriers and help to give the strategies recognition.

All the strategies considered are, in principle, politically independent, but only half of them so far have achieved the sort of practical results (apart from producing a document) which are likely to ensure the continuity of the process in the event of a political change.

Strategies frequently depend on the action of NGOs and the political support of governments, but except in the cases of Petén and Sierra Maestra there has not yet been a sufficient degree of commitment

(legal, social, economic and financial) to guarantee the continuity of the process, in the event of either a) a change of political leadership; b) the loss of international cooperation; or c) the eventual exhaustion of the NGOs' budgets for the projects.

Loss of continuity ceases to be a risk in the cases where:

- target groups either control the process (APTA, Kuna-Yala, Quintana Roo) or are closely involved (Guánica, Pikín-Guerrero, Talamanca);
- a self-financing strategy is being developed (Tambopata, Tortuguero); or
- the government itself is organizing the implementation process (Majé, Petén, Sierra Maestra, Mata Atlántica).

One case worth mentioning in particular is Cuba's Sierra Maestra, where national integration and inter-sectoral cooperation appear to have been achieved. A weakness of the strategy might be its dependence on the government, which would affect it substantially if it had to face either a political change or market competition upsetting established industrial and financial structures.

Participants have found that the free market, driven by short-term competitiveness, provides no better guarantee of a shift towards ecological and industrial

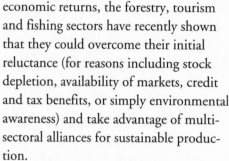

sustainability. Cases such as Petén and Tortuguero, which produced future scenarios as analytical tools, foresee alarming socio-environmental situations occurring within a generation. They suggest that the state intervene with regulatory measures (in the legal, fiscal and credit areas) so as to encourage the development of sustainable production activities, while at the same time, making them competitive.

Institutional Arrangements

The joint participation of government and NGOs is a common feature of all the cases analyzed. One of the clearest results of these processes, which is evident in practically all the cases, is the liaison and coordination between governmental and non-governmental organizations. At least nine of the sub-national strategies constituted the first experiment in their regions in inter-institutional and inter-sectoral coordination to plan the use of natural resources (Amazonia, El Beni, Bocas del Toro, Guánica, Samaná, San Martín, Sierra Nevada, Tambopata and Tortuguero).

All the strategies (except Héroes and Mártires) either have or will have a joint institutional committee responsible for their development, generally under the authority of a government department related to natural resources, and with the participation of local authorities and NGOs. Basic producer groups are repre-

sented on these committees only in Amazonia, Sierra Nevada, Tambopata and in the APTA, Kuna-Yala and Quintana Roo projects.

Regional committees and working groups are also useful tools for integrating the strategies within government planning systems. The members of these committees or groups may be linked to higher levels of government; for instance, the results achieved by the Costa Rica strategy were due to the personal action of experts who took part in its preparation and were later appointed to related government posts.

The Promoting Team: The Engine for the Strategy

Strategies require an engine or driving force. This is usually provided by the technical team rather than an intermediate-level joint institutional committee. Technical teams must be convinced of the feasibility and appropriateness of sustainable development; they must have a degree of commitment beyond the work itself; clear objectives; negotiating abilities and a strong determination to overcome the frequent setbacks and inertia. The ideal technical team is inter-disciplinary and representative of the main interests involved. This is seldom found in any of the cases analyzed, although technicians are frequently delegated by two or three of the main sponsors of each strategy.

One important and positive fact is that these teams are fully national or local (except in Tambopata and Petén), and generally have an office within the working area, which is used as a headquarters by participants. On the other hand, although it is essential that such teams be funded, the necessary financial resources usually cover only a year or two. A further problem, which has been illustrated in several cases, is that the more able and experienced technicians tend to abandon their field work either for family reasons, to look for a better job elsewhere or to join one of the international cooperation agencies. This syndrome also affects programme leaders, who, although they remain involved, gradually distance themselves from field problems.

The strategies which have produced the best results all have in common a strongly committed team to promote the strategy; sometimes one or two key individuals have kept the process going for long periods of time. This kind of personal commitment is more necessary when the process has not yet produced enough results to convince the different sectors of the concrete benefits of the strategy; when participants do benefit, they tend to shift from critical observation to voluntary cooperation, as shown in the cases of APTA, Guánica, Kuna-Yala, Quintana Roo, Pikín-Guerrero, Tambopata and Tortuguero. In these cases, the technical team's energy is gradually matched by the other participants.

Dissemination and Follow-up

Working groups

Joint institutional working groups for the different sectors (agricultural, forestry, tourism, fishing and conservation) were considered in nine cases: Amazonia, APTA, Guánica, Majé, Mata Atlántica, Petén, Samaná, Sierra Maestra and Tortuguero.

Pilot projects

All the strategies (except three) are developing pilot projects in priority areas, in order to promote sustainable production alternatives and to concentrate efforts on concrete actions.

Communication

The mass media were utilized in the cases of Guánica, Petén, San Martín and Tortuguero.

Monitoring and evaluation

A system of participatory monitoring of the process, with measurable indicators, has been established only in Sierra Maestra. El Beni, Petén, Tambopata and Tortuguero have introduced physical indicators (forest coverage) as well as socio-economic indicators (population, family income and production/reinvestment ratios). The APTA, Cinturón Verde,

Pikín-Guerrero, Quintana Roo and Talamanca projects monitor production aspects, while the other cases maintain internal evaluations of projects, but not of processes.

8   International Funding and Cooperation

Funding is an important tool as far as sustainable development is concerned. If processes are to be sustainable, they have to be self-financing. So far, many strategies have depended on external funding. Almost all the cases analyzed have obtained international financial support to prepare the strategies, in proportions varying from 50 per cent in Tambopata to almost 100 per cent in Amazonia, El Beni, Cinturón Verde, Fonseca, Majé, Petén, Pikín-Guerrero, Samaná, Sierra Nevada, San Martín and Talamanca. In all the cases except Guánica, Kuna-Yala, Majé, Petén, Sierra Nevada and Tortuguero, projects report shortages of funds; these are particularly serious in the cases of Samaná, San Martín and Sierra Maestra.

International Cooperation

The analysis shows that strategies, whether already formulated or in the course of drafting and/or implementation, are sufficient in themselves to generate interest among international cooperation agencies. All the strategies prepared financing proposals, which in many cases entailed including the first action plans. Strategies which already included an overall plan of action were presented as proposals to obtain external funding. All the cases, except Cuba, generated interest in some international donor organization.

One possible drawback to international cooperation is that some projects will be designed according to the criteria and priorities of the donor agencies in response to a limited and passing interest. Donor agencies often disregard coordination with other agencies, which may be involved in parallel, more broad-ranging, non-sustainable development programmes. Although donors are gradually achieving a more process-oriented approach, such programmes tend to attract funds with no guarantee of continuity, or else the sustainable development process is reduced to being just a series of project activities which require continuous funding.

National Financial Support

While international technical and financial support is recommended in modest amounts to initiate a process, strategies must make an effort to strengthen their self-financing component. The national and local financial sectors are conspicuous by their absence in practically all these strategy proposal preparation processes.

Reasons for this may include:

- the high professional profile of the work teams involved,
- the initial predominance of conservation aims over economic development objectives, or
- frequently, the presence of international donors, which initially fills the gap.

The cases of Sierra Maestra in Cuba, Guánica in Puerto Rico, Quintana Roo in Mexico and Mata Atlántica in Brazil are exceptions, in that they are more than 90 per cent funded from local and national sources. It is worth noting, moreover, that some of these cases have been among those obtaining the best field results and have proved to be unaffected by political changes occurring in the countries concerned.

9 Limitations of the Analysis

A preliminary analysis of the cases shows that local strategies are effective; that they are, to a large degree, experimental and that we are pioneering new approaches. For this very reason, it is worth trying to extract a few conclusions. However, the limitations of the reviews should also be acknowledged:

a. The processes analyzed are in their initial stages of development. Even

taking into account the positive results referred to previously, the analysis of these strategies must be restricted to the formulation and organization stages, since experience of their implementation is limited (except in the case of Sierra Maestra and the projects).

b. The concepts of sustainable development and strategic planning are new and have not yet permeated all sectors.

c. All these strategies are subject to the influence of strong externalities, which have not always been identified or dealt with.

d. Not enough time has passed for conclusive results about whether the strategies have: set in motion a process of change; correctly identified action priorities; strengthened the local capacity for sustainable development; been adaptive; or been able to be self-sustaining in the long term.

However, the following results appear to be significant enough to be noteworthy at this stage.

10 Main common results

Better Planning

The main achievement to emerge from all the cases analyzed has been the introduction of environmental factors for the first time in planning exercises. In many cases, the strategies also broke new ground with the use of inter-sectoral development planning tools and participatory methodologies.

Greater Capacity

As a result, in all cases there has been a strengthening of the local population's capacity to manage its own resources, a creation of inter- and intra-sectoral coordination structures, and an acceptance of the joint responsibility of NGOs, and civil and community organizations for planning, conservation and development.

Appropriate Technologies

The technical results are still incipient, but promising. Some strategies have served as a framework for new land-use planning schemes. Prospects for conservation of biological diversity and natural resources have improved substantially in all the strategies which have begun to be implemented. Over half the cases have also produced positive results in the forestry sector and in other major productive sectors, such as agriculture, fishing and tourism.

Wherever the production sector has been more involved, better tools have been developed to guarantee that the strategies do not remain a mere planning exercise.

The first technologies for sustainable production are being developed in the cases of APTA, Cinturón Verde, Pikín-Guerrero, Talamanca and in the participatory field projects of the Héroes y Mártires, Petén, Quintana Roo, Sierra Maestra, Sierra Nevada, Tambopata and Tortuguero strategies.

Awareness

All the cases have improved the environmental awareness of the public, the officials involved and local organizations, while some have managed to introduce official environmental education programmes as part of the formal education systems.

11 Main Problems

Reactive Processes

All the local strategies considered in the analysis were initiated as a reaction to problems arising from the degradation of natural resources, with an initial emphasis on the conservation of biological diversity and forest management. Many of the processes began as a response to severely deteriorated socio-environmental situations, whereas strategic planning should be used as a preventive and not just a reactive tool.

Strong Externalities

There is a general concern about how to integrate the strategies into national economic and development policy, and how to integrate the latter in turn into international policies. All the sub-national strategies are subject to strong externalities, particularly of a socio-economic kind, but also political and in some cases military.

Throughout Latin America there are significant constraints to achieving sustainable development, including the detrimental effects of imported economic models, high rates of external debt, structural adjustment policies, and credit policies that support non-sustainable extractive activities. The affected areas become exporters of raw materials with a very low proportion of reinvestment, which adds to the traditional economic undervaluation of natural resources.

The detrimental social effects found in agricultural frontier areas is a further constraint, where population growth is aggravated by immigration from other neighbouring areas.

Limited Capacity

The capacity to respond to these pressures, especially with the degree of urgency required, is at present very limited. There are institutional weaknesses and an insufficient power base to enforce existing standards; additionally, there is the lack of continuity of government programmes, duplication, and lack of coordination among institutions. This is true not only among organizations of the same sector, but also between different government departments; for instance, between those in charge of agriculture and those dealing with natural resources in the cases of El Beni, Mata Atlántica, Samaná, Tambopata and Tortuguero.

Lessons Learned

One very general lesson is that **there is no single recipe** for sustainable development strategies, apart from **adapting to local conditions**. This does not mean that there are no common lessons to be learned. It is interesting to note how projects carried out over several years, thousands of kilometres apart, have reached common conclusions regarding concepts, methods and approaches.

1 The Concept

Processes

The most widely accepted concept is that strategies are **processes** leading towards a comprehensive, complex objective, namely sustainable development. These processes comprise practical, visible activities, while at the same time involving planning activities. Nevertheless, the term 'strategy' can be misinterpreted as a form of long-term plan, governed by a linear, stage-by-stage approach, with an emphasis on producing a bureaucratic document.

In practice it has been found that when a strategy is applied, it becomes influenced and altered by events. Undoubtedly there may be mistakes in the strategy; however, it is wrong to think that by perfecting planning, we might achieve the 'perfect strategy'. This simply does not exist, since reality is always more complex than we imagine. As strategies are implemented, new concepts and ideas evolve. Planning and coordination have to be dynamic and flexible, since conditions are variable and situations change.

Is a Document Necessary?

In view of the diversity of situations analyzed, it is not easy to give a single answer. Some field results appear to suggest that a document is not necessary. For instance, tens of thousands of families occupy hundreds of thousands of hectares of farmable forest areas in APTA in Brazil, in the forests of Quintana Roo in Mexico, in the hills of Sierra Nevada in Colombia or Talamanca in Costa Rica, and in the Kuna-Yala territory of Panama. For years, these people have been involved in a process leading towards the sustainability of production and a self-management capacity, without ever feeling the need to put their plans down in writing, except as a means of obtaining external financing.

In other cases, such as in Petén or in Cuba, the document was necessary to initiate the implementation of the strategies. While most cases have not managed to have their documents officially adopted, they recognize that placing excessive emphasis on a written product can divert valuable time and resources from strategic actions in the field.

The analysis of these 24 experiments suggests that processes should not become obsessed either with documents or planning. All participants agreed that a strategy was much more than a document, although a document was useful for several purposes, such as helping to make a strategy explicit, extracting guidelines which can be officially recognized by governments, helping to establish priorities, and providing a useful tool for socializing concepts and ideas and promoting participation.

Planning/Action

According to the analysis, planning and action should run in parallel; ideally, there will be cross-fertilization between them. Exhaustive planning devoid of action results in a loss of interest and confidence of participants, and reduces the process to committee meetings. Action unrelated to planning, however, may mean that opportunities to work with other sectors and develop common guidelines are missed.

Strategists must both plan and implement. At all levels, they must retain practical – and at least occasional – responsibilities for implementation activities. Similarly, those involved in field action must participate in planning. Field workers who are not aware of the significance of their work within the strategy as a whole tend to lose their enthusiasm and become ineffective.

All the formulation/action processes examined in the review have been in existence for at least five years. The cases which have been most engaged in implementation recommend initiating action simultaneously in different sectors.

Feasibility

Strategies must have attainable objectives and it must be possible to demonstrate their feasibility. For politicians, objectives have to be politically and economically viable; if not, the strategies are left outside government plans. From the communities' point of view, it is essential to **prove** that the economic, social and cultural benefits derived from the conservation of natural resources are of benefit to them.

Scales and Levels

The closer to the ground that strategies are implemented, the greater impact they will have in practice. The World Conservation Strategy and UNCED (1992) have furnished a global conceptual framework for sustainable development. National strategies have introduced an environmental framework for planning. In Latin America, the local strategies are actually putting these concepts into practice.

In Latin America, national strategies have provided a channel for reflection and awareness at government level, but they have produced few concrete results on the ground. Many participants consider them politically and economically non-viable. They were useful only to integrate some conservation objectives into development plans, to provide a basis for reflection on regional development, and to serve as a framework for external assistance.

Local strategies seem to offer better chances of implementation than strategies at the national level. Participation is broader and results are more tangible. Local strategies can be used as appropriate instruments for implementing national strategies. Going one step further in the hierarchical level, some local strategies have sought to apply community strategies, even within a single village, among social groups which best represent different development styles and cultural traditions.

The experience in Latin America supports the principle 'think globally, act locally'. In this sense, decentralization is beneficial to strategies. It also recognizes that sustainable development is not feasible in isolation. Every locality is subject to strong externalities; action has to be taken simultaneously at local and national levels. If the national framework is not amenable to sustainable development, then local strategies can contribute convincing results which can bring about positive changes higher up the scale.

2 Avoiding Loss of Continuity

Internalizing strategies

Except in Cuba and Petén, none of the strategies is an officially sanctioned process linking all sectors of the government. The limited success in this area may be due to the fact that strategies a) have not concentrated on macro-economic and regional development aspects, which are government priorities; b) have been perceived as belonging only to the 'conservation sector' or the domain of the NGOs; or c) do not propose specific actions that identify the roles of each participant and are not accompanied by a plan of action.

Strategies need to be accepted by all the participants, and particularly by the various ministries involved. While the ideal niche would be the Ministry of Planning or equivalent, the strategy document should be prepared with the participation of the greatest possible number of institutions involved in achieving the strategy's objectives. The institutions which need to be considered include those in the economic sector and organizations responsible for promoting credit policies and tax exemptions.

Participants must develop confidence in the process. To achieve this, it is best to initially avoid controversial subjects, to work on issues of consensus, to create

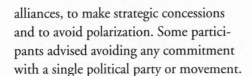

alliances, to make strategic concessions and to avoid polarization. Some participants advised avoiding any commitment with a single political party or movement.

Organizational Bodies

Either a coordinating committee or a supervisory board (inter-institutional) should be set up to maintain the momentum of the strategy, coordinate between the parties and maintain a link with the higher levels of authority. Organizational arrangements have to be dynamic and flexible; it is futile to set up committees before they are required by the dynamics of the strategy. The incentives which keep committees going are a clear definition of roles, a distribution of responsibilities and field results. Written undertakings (agreements) are a good way of backing up cooperation commitments, and for maintenance of joint (technical) institutional working groups.

All the case analyses agree that the strategy cannot depend on a single institution or NGO. In the absence of any inter-sectoral committee or similar body, some strategies rely on particular government departments or even on senior officials, or have formed alliances with national interests likely to provide support. Pressure exerted by donor and cooperation agencies can also be a positive means of influencing national policy.

Technical Teams

With or without formal committees, strategies require a source of energy to keep them going and to motivate the staff. Government bodies may provide the necessary leadership (as in the cases of the national strategies of Cuba, Nicaragua and Peru, or the sub-national strategies of Sierra Maestra, Majé and Petén), but frequently it is the dedication of NGOs or committed teams with charismatic leaders which lie behind the most successful experiments.

It is important to maintain an inter-disciplinary (if possible, inter-institutional) strategy team, and to involve intermediate-level officials and not just senior officials in decisions. It is also important for technical staff to be national citizens. Having a committed field team is fundamental. Field teams have succeeded in maintaining consistency and interest during difficult times. No strategy will succeed if we do not believe in them. Many teams have stated that they never accept part-time members on the strategy team to avoid a division of focus and commitment.

The lack of intermediate, specialized technical staff is a limitation mentioned in all the local cases analyzed. Practically all the strategies have used the human resources of NGOs. This has made a fundamental contribution to sustainable development processes in the region, especially in remote localities where the government's presence is minimal.

Financing the Processes

In order to keep a process moving, there has to be at least a minimum amount of resources to ensure support for the work of the strategy team, and to provide sufficient, flexible budgets to cover workshops, exchanges, small publications and seed funds for local initiatives. Where these minimum resources have not been available, strategies have had to be content with very limited opportunities or have been unable to carry on. Many participants agree that it is not even worth setting the machinery in motion for a strategy with insufficient, inconsistent or fragmented budgets.

All the strategies, except in Cuba and partly in Brazil, have been heavily dependent on external funds. A few cases are contemplating adding to the local/national financial capacity and eventually doing without international cooperation. In this respect, some cases (Kuna-Yala Pikín, Tortuguero) went through some 'bridging' periods of up to a year without external financing. The experience was tough, particularly for the technical teams, but the processes eventually came out all the stronger. The local and national promoters of the strategies had to make up for these shortages and in the process

their awareness and understanding of the process actually improved. The technical teams also found themselves having to reconsider their priorities and to concentrate on the more relevant aspects.

Strengthening Local Capacity

The prime achievement of formulating a strategy is not the production of a consensus document, but rather generating the necessary participation to internalize its recommendations and strengthening the local capacity for implementing strategy actions. The strategy team should not try to resolve all the problems that arise, but should make use of existing organizations, strengthen them in their sustainable development objectives and endorse existing initiatives. In other words it should act as a catalyst, a guide and a supervisor for the process, taking advantage of and strengthening **existing capacity** in the region, so that the national and local players can eventually assume ownership.

The capacity required is organizational and technical as well as economic. It is important for strategies to establish their financial self-sustainability on the basis of local sources, the development of supervisory mechanisms for sustainable development, and the concept of an economic strategy which allows these areas a role in national development and ensures their integration and competitiveness in the long term.

3 Participation

The Importance of Participation

Strategies belong to everyone, not just their promoters. Sustainable development involves the whole of society. All the cases point to the fact that broad participation and the involvement of government, private, social and NGO sectors in the analyses, proposals and implementation of programmes are key factors in guaranteeing the successful outcome of a strategy process. In practice this participation takes the form of **shared responsibility**; in this sense, participation is more than just **consultation**.

Participation in Practice

The parties involved usually have no previous experience of participatory planning. This inexperience was reflected in the difficulty encountered in generating an inter-sectoral vision of problems and their solutions, and also in the difficulty of sustaining the interest of participants in the continuation of the process. People need incentives to participate in a strategy. One way of doing this is to look for a point of consensus in the beginning, and to focus on some feature on which all (or practically all) potential participants can agree.

Participation will be stronger if it is initiated right from the start of the process, with shared responsibility for the results. Another important aspect is that all participants must have a clear notion of their specific role in the process. This clear definition of roles is fundamental if internal conflicts are to be avoided. In general, a better response was achieved by participants who had clear planning objectives.

One way of applying this principle is to gather together potential participants in order to produce a common assessment of issues and needs. Participants can then contribute information pertaining to their specialized fields. This makes it easier to identify information, avoids duplication, makes use of local capacity and creates a shared responsibility for the result.

The Limitations of Participation

Participation also has its limitations. Any serious participatory planning takes time and patience if it is to be done properly. As mentioned earlier, participation tends to bring latent conflicts to the surface, but it also prevents them getting worse. Last, it is impossible and impractical to include everyone; the breadth and depth of the process will depend on the scale and focus of each strategy. For instance, at the level of a department or province, the participation of target groups should be restricted to representatives of local organizations and should not be open to individuals in the communities.

Some cases were stalled because of too much participation at different levels with differing interests. At the level of community strategies, while target groups should participate fully, the presence of senior officials who may be pursuing specific political interests may hold up the process. Participation can have several layers with the same objective; the upper layer of participation establishes the general framework for the region, while the lower layer implements practical measures among the target groups. The resulting actions reflect the participation of both these layers.

4   Implementation of Strategies

Mistakes

Mistakes are a basic element of learning, which means that a working strategy should clearly identify mistakes and learn from them. Some participants expressed the view that there was a right, and even an obligation, to err. There should be no fear of mistakes and the risk of being wrong should not be allowed to inhibit action. Sharing and talking about mistakes is a good way of learning and helping others.

Communications

One mistake to learn from is the relative inability of all the strategies to communicate effectively with all sectors of society. Participants make enormous efforts to maintain the consistency of the processes and to keep participants' interest alive, but most forgot to keep the public informed of progress through the mass media. Equally, strategies have not been presented in a practical, simple way, so as to convince the public of the tangible benefits they offer and to show governments how the strategies can facilitate their task.

Representatives? Leaders?

The official authorities in charge are not necessarily representative of their communities, nor do they necessarily pass on information to the public. In Petén, for instance, where electoral absenteeism was as high as 80 per cent and mayors were deemed not representative of their communities, the projects began working with assistant mayors in the villages, who have often been in their jobs for as long as ten years.

At the local level, some of the cases (Guánica, Kuna-Yala, Petén, Tortuguero) called attention to the unsatisfactory representative qualities of many local leaders, who participated in the formulation of strategies and action plans without

informing their communities. Some communities remained closed to the strategies until the technical teams began negotiating with them directly. The lesson here is that a more direct contact should be sought with the communities, not only through their leaders, but through a forum of participation involving all sectors. Most communities have organizing bodies, in sectors such as sport, health, development, education or cooperatives, in addition to their local authorities. Experience shows that the strategies can set up a liaison committee in each community which is representative of all community groups.

Working with Communities

In local strategies, it is the communities which guarantee the implementation and continuity of the process. All the cases report that commitments with the communities have to be fulfilled efficiently and expeditiously if credibility is not to be lost.

Working with the communities is a complex task. Their interest in participating is won through practical actions, not plans. Actions emerge from a process of self assessment by the community. It has been found that in most cases the communities relegate the conservation of natural resources to a secondary level. Several strategies were started with social and infrastructure projects (for example, in Cinturón Verde with waste recycling; in Samaná with beach cleaning; in Tortuguero with drinking water and in Majé with a food safety scheme).

The tools used most successfully are pilot projects, credit facilities through local banks, exchanges of experience among peasants, the participation of women and the extracurricular work of teachers. Attention has also been drawn to the value of training peasants as a development process compared with the more traditional methods of agricultutral extension.

The technical issues can be solved, however; the difficult decisions are those which require a change in people's behaviour and attitudes. All agreed that the pace and priorities of communities have to be respected. The main lesson is the need to **start from the community's requirements and respond.**

Strategies for Sustainability in Latin America

Central America

1   National Strategy, Costa Rica
2   National Strategy, Nicaragua
3   Kuna-Yala, Panama
4   Majé-Bayano, Panama
5   Petén, Guatemala
6   Tortuguero, Costa Rica
7   Héroes y Mártires, Nicaragua
8   Talamanca, Costa Rica

Caribbean

9   Guánica, Puerto Rico
10   Bahía de Samaná, Dominican Republic
11   Sierra Maestra, Cuba

South America

12   Amazonia, Ecuador
13   Sierra Nevada, Colombia
14   Mata Atlántica, Brazil
15   Tambopata-Candamo, Peru

Part 2:
Case Studies

Case Studies: Central America

National Strategy, Costa Rica
National Strategy, Nicaragua
Kuna-Yala, Panama
Majé-Bayano, Panama
Petén, Guatemala
Tortuguero, Costa Rica
Héroes y Martires, Nicaragua
Talamanca, Costa Rica

Costa Rica

Strategy for Sustainable Development

ROLANDO MENDOZA, NATIONAL UNIVERSITY;
CARLOS QUESADA, UNIVERSITY OF COSTA RICA
AND VIVIENNE SOLÍS, IUCN–ORMA

1 Introduction

Costa Rica's Conservation Strategy for
Sustainable Development (ECODES) was
the first effort at a national level to link
conservation and development. It was
both a response to the growing concern
about threats to the environment and a
timely reply to international calls for
sustainable development. At present
(1995), many of the main guidelines of
ECODES have been incorporated in the
new government's political programme
(1994–1998), even though the strategy
has not yet been officially adopted.

The strategy process began during the
term of office of former president Oscar
Arias (1986–1990), with the support of
the Ministry of Natural Resources, Energy
and Mines (MIRENEM), which was set
up in the same period. It also obtained the
backing of various ministries, universities
and autonomous institutions, and the
participation of a number of non-governmental organizations. The document was
published by MIRENEM in 1990

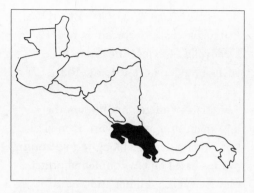

COSTA RICA
Population: 3,000,000
Land area: 50,500 km^2
Population density: 59.4 inhab/km^2

(Quesada Mateo, C. (1990). ECODES: Estrategia de Conservación para el Desarrollo Sostenible de Costa Rica. MIRENEM, San José, Costa Rica).

The strategy offered not just another document proposing environmental plans, but rather a dynamic, long-term planning process based on environmental principles. ECODES did not attempt to substitute more short-term national or regional planning efforts, but rather was intended to provided a reference framework to ensure that these planning processes combined the objectives of conservation and socio-economic development.

The subsequent government (1990–1994) recognized ECODES as a significant reference document but didn't adopt it as a working basis for environmental decisions. Despite the lack of formal relations between ECODES and the government planning departments in this period, it is interesting to note that a number of national programmes were compatible with the strategy's guidelines, even though they had no direct connection with ECODES. Examples include the National System of Protected Areas (SINAC), the Forest Wildlife Act, the Forest Action Plan and the introduction of environmental subjects in formal education.

ECODES, and especially the process in which it originated, represents a significant milestone in the history of Costa Rica's search for a sustainable society. The present government (1994–98), led by José M Figueres, has adopted sustainable development as the guideline of its development policies. Taking its inspiration from the philosophy and proposals contained in ECODES, and more recently in Agenda 21, the new government's first act was to give wide publicity to a political programme aimed at sustainable development, which included 70 major plans covering all socio-economic development sectors and the conservation of natural resources. The most significant of these policies and practical measures are outlined on page 44. They include raising environmental rights to constitutional status, the creation of a system of conservation areas covering the whole of the country, new industrial and energy policies, guidelines for agricultural development and forestry, the creation of public participation forums and the establishment of the National Coordinating Body for Sustainable Development (SINADES).

2 Scope and Objectives

Costa Rica's ECODES was conceptually rooted in the latest thinking in conservation and development in the late 1980s, and was Costa Rica's first effort to develop a strategy of action in the field of conservation for development based on a systematic, comprehensive and long-term

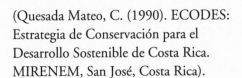

approach. The fundamental principle underlying ECODES is that sustainable development has to be the country's long-term objective.

In 1994, many of the guiding principles of ECODES had been incorporated in the political programme of the new government. The following fundamental objective was taken from President Figueres's document (Gobierno de Costa Rica y Consejo de la Tierra, 1994. Desarollo Sostenible, Costa Rica: el compromiso es realizable. Foro Internaciol "Del Bosque a la Sociedad". San José, 9-11 May, 1994).

> "To establish guidelines for government action at national level, aimed at improving the quality of life of the citizens of Costa Rica, and managing productive and economic aspects in harmony with natural resources and the environment."

Specific objectives (in summary form) include:

- active, concerted participation by the government and society;
- a new institutional framework favouring decentralization;
- land-use planning;
- combating poverty;
- promoting information and education concerning sustainable development;
- investigating the use and enhancement of natural resources;
- promoting the recycling of materials and avoiding pollution;
- making the development of major infrastructure subordinate to its usefulness to sustainable development and minimizing its environmental impact;
- promoting sustainable forms of farming;
- promoting appropriate technologies and reviewing consumption practices;
- ensuring that trade incorporates environmental criteria; and
- creating a national fund for sustainable development.

3 Relationship to Development Planning

Although ECODES has not yet been officially adopted, its influence has been significant. It served as a starting point for establishing Costa Rica's National System of Protected Areas, Forest Wildlife Act, Forest Action Plan and Environmental Education Master Plan.

ECODES guidelines also inspired the last government's political programme, which included 70 major plans and gave rise to a considerable number of legal procedures. The main innovations were granting constitutional status to environmental rights, creating a nationwide system of conservation areas, signing inter-sectoral agreements, ratifying international agreements, and establishing SINADES.

4 Initial Development

Despite the country's conservation efforts, the rapid destruction of the environment and the lack of environmental policies linked to the development process caused concern among professional groups in Costa Rica. The government of Oscar Arias set up MIRENEM by executive decree, which reflected the government's firm intention to ensure proper management of the country's natural resources.

The 17th General Assembly of the World Conservation Union (IUCN), held in Costa Rica in 1987, provided timely encouragement for the idea of forging a national conservation strategy for sustainable development. Five international NGOs promised their financial and technical support for the undertaking, namely IUCN, Conservation International, Conservation Foundation, The Nature Conservancy and the Worldwide Fund for Nature (WWF).

MIRENEM acted as a centre of operations and provided the process with technical support. It also supplied initial funding pending the arrival of the international support which the project had attracted. A strategy management team (director, executive assistant and secretary) drafted methodological guidelines and coordinated the process.

One of the first steps taken in developing the strategy was to convene a group of 17 professionals, who were put in charge of the different sectors planned for ECODES. Each coordinator worked with a select group (between four and ten) of professionals. In the course of the process they acted as experts, with the task of preparing a sectoral proposal as part of the overall strategy. These work teams held meetings and organized workshops and other activities, meeting in plenary session from time to time with the other teams in charge of neighbouring strategy sectors.

A technical committee and a steering committee operated throughout the process. They comprised some 40 people of the highest professional calibre, who had each demonstrated experience and commitment. The persons chosen for the technical committee had training and experience in their respective sectors, while the management committee included professionals with a broad-ranging view. The national governmental institutions and NGOs linked to the country's development were represented on both committees.

Three workshops were held during the preparatory phase of the strategy. These were attended by a team from each sector as well as by the technical and management committees. The sectoral teams' systems methodology provided generic reference terms for the different sectors and helped to find a common language to analyze the key issues, problems and mandate of the different sectors. The workshops were a useful exercise in participation and inter-disciplinary work, and provided an opportunity to discuss and exchange views on major conservation and development issues.

This work led to the preparation of the First National Congress on the Conservation Strategy for Sustainable Development, which offered an opportunity to improve the process prior to the preparation of the consolidated document. All four presidential candidates attended the congress, which ensured that the theme of the strategy and sustainable development was firmly on the political agenda for the forthcoming elections and would therefore achieve a high level of public recognition.

Since then, the present government has set up SINADES, with the objective of ensuring the integration of all national policies and action for sustainable development. SINADES includes a National Council, advisory technical committees, a Public Participation Council and a Foundation for Sustainable Development.

5 Implementation and Results

ECODES provided the starting point for a number of major initiatives in the country, such as setting up the Biodiversity Institute, preparing the National Energy Plan (following preliminary efforts to encourage energy savings and efficiency), and instituting the Forest Wildlife Act, the Forest Action Plan, and the Master Plan for Environmental Education. In general, there was a strengthening of existing initiatives. One such example was the National Parks Service, a programme initiated in 1970 which gradually evolved into a decentralized system of conservation areas. The programme was proposed in 1990 and became official in 1994.

Successive governments provided varying degrees of support for the strategy. Nevertheless, the seeds sown by ECODES in 1990 – and the interest and commitment in favour of sustainable development by all those who had helped to launch it – survived and grew, eventually flourishing after 1994, when political circumstances improved.

Notable features of the government's 1994–98 programme include:

- granting constitutional status to environmental rights;
- the creation of a system of conservation areas covering the whole of the country;
- the ratification of the UNCED Rio agreements and the creation of SINADES;
- the fight against poverty;
- the creation of citizen participation forums;
- land-use planning;

- limitation of the agricultural sector's environmental impact;
- regulation of CO_2 emissions;
- elimination of lead in fuels; and
- a public information campaign on matters related to development.

6 Lessons Learned

Factors in favour of the strategy process include:

- the channelling of moral and financial support, and the degree of environmental awareness achieved by individuals prepared to work as a team, acted as catalysts and contributed to the success of the process;
- the participation of local professionals, familiar with the national situation and committed to change;
- the technical and inter-disciplinary emphasis, leading to a proper inter-sectoral analysis based on systems analysis; and

- the international image generated by the process. The government's explicit policy in favour of sustainable development has proved to be a significant attraction for the tourism sector and for international cooperation.

Factors against the strategy process include:

- ECODES was set up hurriedly with an already overworked team;
- from 1990 to 1994, the strategy was limited to the extent that it was not accepted as a major planning objective; and
- when ECODES was first formulated and in subsequent years (1987–1993), there was little institutional commitment to it. This was due partly to political changes, but also to the fact that it began as the initiative of a single ministry (MIRENEM).

Lessons learned from the process include:

- a strategy is a way of moving towards the future. It provides a method of anticipating scenarios and situations in order to prevent future detrimental impacts. The participatory process required a great deal of learning. Inter-disciplinary cooperation enabled colleagues in different departments to learn together and helped individuals to recognize the other person's point of view and arrive at a consensus through dialogue;

- changes of government should not mean the end of the process. Even though there was not always formal continuity from one administration to the next, one of the most positive outcomes in the case of Costa Rica was the creation of informal networks;
- as outlined in Quesada Mateo (1990): "There is a need to formulate a strategy to serve as a reference framework for future development plans, although this requires a greater degree of political maturity on the part of policy-makers and society as a whole, with regard to the understanding and significance of ECODES"; and
- the development of an environmental policy in Costa Rica is due as much to the process initiated by ECODES on a national level, as to the encouragement for sustainable development policies derived from international and Costa Rican commitments at the Rio summit.

7 Chronology

1976   Costa Rica 2000 Symposium, the first national forum at which aspects of development and the conservation of natural resources are discussed.

1982   Publication of the *Environmental Profile of Costa Rica.*

1986   Establishment of Ministry of Natural Resources, Energy and Mines (MIRENEM) by executive decree.

1987   Appointment of a director for ECODES and start of preparations for the strategy. International support obtained for the initiation of the process (US$ 110,000). 17th IUCN General Assembly in Costa Rica.

1988   Various public information activities related to the preparation of the strategy at national and international level and participation in several official ministerial committees. First Congress of the National Conservation Strategy for Sustainable Development (public meeting held in the National Theatre).

1989   Follow-up activities and completion of ECODES sector coordination. Beginning of pre-electoral period.

1990   New government of president Rafael Angel Calderón (1990–1994). Publication of National Conservation Strategy document and of the report on the First Congress.

1991   Initiation of Forest Action Plan for Costa Rica. Publication of Master Plan for Environmental Education for Costa Rica. Completion of National Biodiversity Institute. Establishment of National Environmental Education Commission by government decree following ECODES recommendations and the Master Plan for Environmental Education.

1992   Approval of new Forest Wildlife Conservation Act.

1994   The government of President J M Figueres proclaims sustainable development as the basis of its political programme for 1994–1998, including 70 major guidelines for national development, and a considerable number of practical measures. Establishment of SINADES. Approval of Conservation Areas Act, covering the whole of the national territory, and initiation of decentralization in the management and conservation of natural resources.

1995   Environmental rights of Costa Rican citizens raised to constitutional status.

Nicaragua

National Conservation Strategy for Sustainable Development

BAYARDO SERRANO, MARENA,
WITH THE ASSISTANCE OF ALBERTO SALAS, IUCN

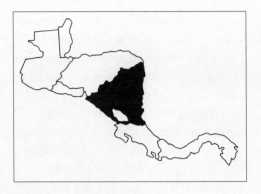

NICARAGUA
Population: 3,000,000
Land area: 148,000 km²
Population density: 21 inhab/km²

1 Introduction

Compared with other countries in the area, Nicaragua possesses substantial natural resources in the form of fertile land, forestry resources, water resources, fisheries, minerals and scenery. This major potential could generate a diversified supply of raw materials and services if it were comprehensively and sustainably managed. More diversified production could provide the basis for a sound, creative and dynamic relation with world markets while satisfying the basic needs of the population. So far, however, development policies have run into considerable difficulties when attempting to take full advantage of the diversified, complex and generous supply of natural resources available.

The way in which natural resources have been used has caused serious degradation in the country's ecosystems, through water pollution and shortages, fertile soil erosion and deforestation. In view of the social and environmental situation currently facing the people of Nicaragua, there is an urgent need to adopt and implement a strategy for sustainable development. This strategy should resolve existing problems, while undertaking to mobilize the country's full potential. This will help to achieve economic growth and satisfy the essential requirements of the population and of national development from a medium- and long-term perspective. Such a strategic requirement must at the same time remain open to the profound technological, economic and political changes which have occurred in the world.

In 1990, the Government of Nicaragua undertook to formulate its National Conservation Strategy for Sustainable Development. This initiative coincided with the Forest Action Plan and sought to secure the broadest possible participation of all Nicaraguan sectors. The national team placed special emphasis on the need to involve all local authorities, recognizing their independent status and seeking to share responsibility throughout Nicaraguan society.

The strategy was approved by the central government in 1992 by presidential decree, pending the submission and approval of the Environmental Action Plan (PAANIC) to initiate implementation. The Environmental Action Plan received the financial support of the Danish International Development Agency (DANIDA) in 1993. Nevertheless

at present (1995), the strategy has lost momentum in terms of governmental policy. This is due to the disbanding of the technical team, which had acted as the driving force behind the strategy, and because the task of following up the strategy was not delegated to the recently-created Ministry for Natural Resources (MARENA).

2   Objectives and Approach

From the start, Nicaragua's National Conservation Strategy for Sustainable Development included the notion of regional planning as a basic means of achieving sustainability. The general objective of the strategy is to establish a sustainable development model, which will promote economic growth and satisfy the basic needs of the population and of future generations, on the basis of the broadest possible democratic participation, social justice, conservation of the environment and the rational use of natural resources.

Specific objectives may be summarized as follows:

- helping to eliminate poverty, and to improve the living standards and quality of life of the majority of the population, by improving the quality of the environment;
- enhancing democracy by strengthening local government institutions and

public participation in environmental management;

- preserving biodiversity and the viability of ecosystems;
- exploiting natural resources rationally and sustainably;
- increasing the productive supply of goods and services for domestic consumption, especially basic products for the population, and reducing the dependence on oil for energy;
- diversifying exports; and
- decentralizing administration and including the areas of the Atlantic coast.

3 Relationship to Development Planning

From the outset, the strategy incorporated the notion of land-use planning and closer links with the agricultural, tourism and financial sectors. Another important aspect has been the creation of Environmental Units by local authorities.

The strategy was approved by presidential decree in 1992, subject to PAANIC being completed prior to implementation. It was submitted to the international community in an effort to seek the necessary support for priority actions. In 1993, it received financial support from the Danish government.

4 Initial Development

In 1990, the Government of Nicaragua, with the financial support of the Swedish Government, acting through the Swedish International Development Authority (SIDA), agreed to launch the Forest Action Plan for Nicaragua (PAFNIC). The technical unit which was set up to prepare the plan insisted that PAFNIC could not and should not be considered as an isolated forest scheme, but rather as an inter-sectoral responsibility and task, which would be an integral part of national planning. In the light of past experience (a Forest Action Plan had been established in 1985 but never put into practice), it was recognized that, if PAFNIC was to succeed, it had to be part of a broader environmental plan, which in turn would follow the guidelines of a conservation strategy for sustainable development.

At the same time as the importance of territorial planning was recognized, it was also understood that participation was needed at different levels. In this respect, the participation of municipal councils has been a key component.

A national consultation process was organized, involving 143 municipalities from all over the country, local NGOs, departmental delegates of the central government, representatives of Catholic and Evangelical churches, members of the resistance and demobilized members of the Sandinista army. The process provided an opportunity for people to become acquainted with local concerns and initiatives, which were subsequently incorporated in the national proposal.

The strategy team held another series of meetings with technicians, professional associations, indigenous groups, women, journalists, lawyers and others. Many matters were discussed in order to work out a major proposal on a national scale. At the end of this very broad-ranging national exercise, the main problems identified by the population were deforestation, water shortage and pollution, and the lack of environmental education programmes.

Information was gathered and sorted, and the team then returned to each municipality for a second workshop. There participants had the opportunity to review the information processed by the work team. Simultaneously, the unit in charge of formulating the National Conservation Strategy for Sustainable Development and the Forest Action Plan for Nicaragua (ECOT-PAF) organized eight seminars on the identification and formulation of projects, with the support of the Finnish International Development Agency (FINNIDA). The seminars were attended by councillors, town hall officials, NGO delegates, representatives of universities, farmers' associations, women and others.

The strategy proposed a series of measures in all development sectors, as well as 19 conservation and sustainable development programmes (PCODES) as an operational basis for the scheme. These priority programmes were divided into three groups: changes in production, social transformation and support programmes.

5 Implementation and Results

PAANIC constitutes the formal mechanism for strategy implementation. At present it is being developed with the financial support of DANIDA. This is achieving other results, including the following:

- the central government has prepared and approved the strategy, the land-use planning scheme and the Forest Action Plan;
- environmental and ecological development committees have been organized in the municipalities and departments;
- with the support of MARENA, municipal authorities and the Ministry of Education, several municipalities have set up ecological brigades, with the participation of primary and secondary school students;
- Nicaraguan NGOs have adopted the strategy, land-use planning scheme, PAFNIC and PAANIC as their own, and use them as guiding principles for action;

- the stock-breeding sector and cooperatives of farmers with small, medium and large farms have begun the reforestation of their properties;
- the mass media are playing a fundamental role in environmental policy; and
- there has been an increased national awareness of the need to preserve and make rational use of natural resources.

6   Lessons Learned

The active participation of the Nicaraguan people has been useful in furthering the strategy. Perhaps the main lesson learned in this area has been the need to work together from the start. In this sense, participation must be activated when the first formulation steps are taken. Another positive effect of broad participation has been the adoption of the strategy by local authorities, and by parliamentary and other government bodies.

The more negative aspects have included structural adjustment policies and economic policy in general, which have at times distorted the strategy's development. Other negative factors have been institutional weakness and the difficult political situation in Nicaragua.

All these factors are summed up in two basic concerns expressed by the work team. One is the impact which international economic policies may have on the development of the strategy, and the other is the absence of an ECOT-PAF follow-up unit. The lack of such a unit has brought about the present inertia in the strategy, since the new Ministry of Natural Resources has not incorporated the strategy as a guideline for its policies.

7   *Chronology*

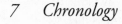

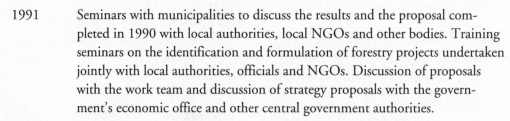

1990   Establishment of the Coordinating Unit. Recruitment of national specialists, development of national consultation, municipal workshops, government processing of information, seminars with government bodies.

1991   Seminars with municipalities to discuss the results and the proposal completed in 1990 with local authorities, local NGOs and other bodies. Training seminars on the identification and formulation of forestry projects undertaken jointly with local authorities, officials and NGOs. Discussion of proposals with the work team and discussion of strategy proposals with the government's economic office and other central government authorities.

1992   Preparation of final documents and submission to government authorities, both local and national. Approval of the strategy by the government and submission of the proposals to international organizations.

1993   Implementation of some FAP projects. Initial formulation of PAANIC, discussions with local authorities and submission of the plan to the central government.

1994   DANIDA finances the implementation of PAANIC.

1995   The disbanding of the technical team, which was the driving force for the strategy, prevents any follow-up with the recently-created Ministry of Natural Resources (MARENA).

Kuna-Yala, Panama

Sustainability for Comprehensive Development

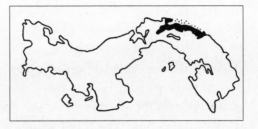

OTONIEL GONZÁLEZ, PEMASKY, WITH THE ASSISTANCE OF VIVIENNE SOLÍS, IUCN

KUNA-YALA, PANAMA
Population: 47,000
Land area: 320,800 ha + 365 small islands
Ecological zones: tropical forest, lime stone islands and reefs
Main economic activities: fishing, agriculture, tourism

1 Introduction

In 1925, the Kuna revolution led to the granting of an indigenous territory called Comarca, which remained part of Panama and was officially recognized in 1953. The territory of Kuna-Yala, on the eastern coast of Panama, is made up of 365 islands (50 of which are inhabited), situated in the Caribbean, in addition to other territory on the coast and in the hinterland. Kuna-Yala, with 47,000 inhabitants, is one of the few remaining indigenous territories in Panama.

Since 1980, the Kuna-Yala people have made considerable effort to oppose the destruction of the forest and natural resources in their territory. For the Kuna people, the forest represents a source of great benefits, including the protection of their aquifers, reefs, fishing, medicines and supplies. They feel that "without the forest, human survival would not be possible". For this reason the forest resource constitutes the focal point of the strategy. The Kuna have kept intact some 80 per cent of the forests in their territory,

compared with only 30 per cent in the rest of Panama.

In 1983, the Association of Kuna Employees (AEK) proposed the Ecological Programme for the Management of the Forest Areas of Kuna-Yala (PEMASKY). This reflected the Kuna people's desire to organize in defence of their environmental resources. The programme was approved by the Kuna General Council, and has become the main driving force behind the plan to achieve a local conservation strategy for sustainable development in Kuna territory. The strategy aims to provide full protection for an area of 100,000 hectares and to manage the territory's forests and lands sustainably, so as to improve the quality of life for present and future Kuna generations.

Since 1983, with the endorsement of the Kuna General Council, agreements have been approved whereby the government undertakes to support the Kuna people's sustainable development activities planned for the strategy. The national government has drawn up a Forest Action Plan, which includes the strategy among its main guidelines. The Kuna community has received the support of NGOs which have taken an interest in the process, such as the Fundación Panamá, ANCON and others.

Funding for the forestry component of the strategy was approved in 1993 by the

International Timber Trade Organization (ITTO) and the Government of Panama through the National Institute for Renewable Natural Resources (INRENARE). A biodiversity inventory is also being completed. In 1994, the government approved the establishment of the full 100,000-hectare reserve proposed for the strategy. Many other activities have been carried out in the areas of training, dissemination and environmental education.

The activities proposed for the strategy have a very good chance of obtaining financial support, although funding will depend on the results produced in this first stage of implementation. On the other hand, the strategy might have benefited from more participation in the formulation process. In addition, there are still problems arising from the attribution of responsibilities, lack of coordination and a poor exchange of information with other NGOs and with some communities. Frequent changes of government have also had a negative effect on local organization. Since 1994, however, these problems are gradually being overcome.

2   Objectives and Approach

The basic goal of the strategy is to support initiatives for the protection of environmental and natural resources in the Kuna territory that will ensure the sustainable use of the forest and improve the living standards of the Kuna people. The strategy is a response to the imminent danger of losing the forest resource through deforestation caused by the introduction of settlers and peasants from the central provinces of the country.

Despite the fact that the forest component has been given greater attention within the process, the strategy includes other important aspects for development and for improving the quality of life of the territory's inhabitants, including land-use planning, activities for the protection of water basins, protection of forest wildlife, agroforestry and improvement of the internal economy.

3   Relationship to Development Planning

The Kuna people have set up the Kuna General Council, which makes decisions and discusses actions to be taken. The Council is made up of 200 official delegates, with three delegates from each community and three territorial chiefs acting as the highest authority. Technicians prepare proposals that are submitted to the Council for approval. The strategy's technical team submitted drafts on three occasions to the Kuna General Council, which approved the document on the third submission.

At present (1995), there is a fairly close relation to the policy of the national government. In Panama, INRENARE is the body in charge of monitoring, protecting and managing the country's natural resources. It was this institution which coordinated the implementation of the Forest Action Plan for Panama. This national planning exercise incorporated the sustainability strategy for the comprehensive development of Kuna-Yala as part of its guidelines. In 1994, at the request of the Kuna-Yala people, the state declared 100,000 hectares within the territory a protected area.

4   Initial Development

As outlined at the beginning of this chapter, the indigenous territory of Comarca was recognized in 1953. The Kuna-Yala community now has its own legislation, language and religion.

Before the arrival of NGOs, and prior to the launching of the PEMASKY programme in 1983, decisions were made by government institutions. This has now changed, and direct consultations are held with organized groups in charge of programming projects for the benefit of indigenous communities. The strategy for the conservation of the Kuna-Yala forest was planned from the start without state interference; that is, it was an initiative that originated entirely within the Kuna community. Following the inception of the project in 1983, serious problems with funding arose during the period of the dictatorship in Panama. It was difficult to sign agreements, for instance, or to follow up any attempts to implement the project. The situation has now improved, however, and there is a direct link with national government policy.

At the beginning, the PEMASKY programme was run by a group of eleven local technicians (specializing in forestry, agronomy, architecture and topography), who constituted the work team responsible for preparing the basic document. This group now recognizes that the document was prepared without sufficient grassroots participation by the Kuna people. Nevertheless, the project team briefed the Kuna General Council twice a year on the progress with strategy preparation. The document was eventually approved by Council. Other measures were later implemented as part of the programme in the field of environmental education, which gave the rest of the population a better idea of what was being proposed for the strategy.

Although there are several Kuna NGOs, only the PEMASKY programme obtained the official recognition of the Kuna General Council. The other organizations have participated in the process, but only through indirect consultation.

At the beginning of the process the idea of formulating a strategy received international support. The main organizations involved were WWF ($150,000), the MacArthur Foundation ($50,000), and the Interamerican Foundation (IAF, $50,000). When the proposal document was prepared, several countries expressed an interest in providing support. Japan, the US and the ITTO sent missions to the area and have all supported the initiative in some form or other. At present the Kuna vision of the project has been accepted, but at the beginning there was some fear among the Kuna people that these outside bodies might interfere with proposed strategy activities, one such possibility arising in the case of Japanese support and the marketing of timber. The project leaders consider that it was understood by the ITTO that the purpose of the project was not to commercialize the timber, but to carry out a basic study aimed at guaranteeing the conservation of the forest resource.

5 Implementation and Results

The strategy includes activities scheduled for immediate implementation which were given priority in a plan of action. The strategy as a whole will be implemented under the PEMASKY programme, with the advice of technicians working for the Forest Action Plan coordinated by the INRENARE. Current activities include an inventory of forest resources, research into biodiversity, agroforestry projects, indigenous medicine and environmental education. The local capacity for conservation has improved substantially. The community's own technicians have taken an active part in preparing and implementing the strategy guidelines.

In 1994, the national government established a 100,000-hectare reserve in the territory at the Kuna people's request. This notwithstanding, the achievements of this project in practice have been severely hampered by political and economic problems. The collection of funds has never been properly organized, while local NGOs have proliferated and have in some form or other diverted funds originally collected for PEMASKY. Once again, the frequent changes of government have also had a substantial effect.

The main tools used for management are:

- land-use capacity plans emphasizing the protection of waterways and forests;
- inter-institutional working groups (forestry and conservation sectors);
- training of project technicians and seminars for local forestry officials;
- systematic environmental education;
- frequent meetings with communities, leaders and grassroots organizations;
- requests to international sponsors for funds;

- development of self-financing plans based on ecological tourism activities and other productive activities (including the sale of handicraft products); and
- review of the strategy every three years.

6 Lessons Learned

Aspects in favour of the process include:

- the interest and dedication shown by local technicians in the formulation of the document, and the support of professionals from foreign universities;
- incorporation of ideas from the cultural perspective of the Kuna people, with those concerned taking a direct part in preparing and implementing the strategy;
- achievement of a consensus among the parties (communities, users and government bodies);
- approval of the plan by the national government and incorporation of the strategy within the Forest Action Plan for Panama; and
- definition and planning of short- and medium-term scenarios based on standards for the use of natural resources.

Main factors against the strategy process include:

- the leaders of the Kuna community were not brought in from the start. The

technical team planned the strategy's guidelines without any proper consultation, even though the guidelines were approved by the Kuna General Council. The basic document would have been more complete if the community had been involved from the first stages of drafting. Permanent consultations need to be held with the communities involving the grassroots leaders;

- some ecological concepts and terms are incomprehensible to the target groups;
- lack of forestry technicians familiar with the Kuna cultural reality; and
- the strategy is almost entirely limited to the forestry sector, while insufficient effort has been made to develop other aspects linked to biodiversity and human development.

The main lessons learned are:

- the participation of the population at large in strategy formulation, not mere consultation through the leaders, is important as a means of obtaining public support and assistance in later stages;
- the strategy must be developed by a local team. This will identify and strengthen the Kuna people's own initiatives in the area of sustainable development; and
- the indigenous communities are fully able to conduct a process based on appropriate guidelines for the management of their own natural resources.

7   *Chronology*

1925   The Kuna-Yala, through a revolution, obtain the autonomy of their territory (Comarca).

1953   The Government of Panama officially recognizes the Comarca by official act

1983   AEK establishes PEMASKY, which is approved by the Kuna General Council.

1987   Completion of the document (Kuna-Yala Management Plan) covering the basic conservation aspects of the territory's natural resources. The management plan is the beginning of the process of preparing the strategy. The document is approved by the Kuna General Council.

1989   Invasion of the Republic of Panama by the United States. First revision of the management plan. Cooperation agreements are concluded with various institutions, national NGOs and donor organizations.

1991   Second revision of the management plan and cooperation agreement with the INRENARE.

1993   Funding obtained for a general evaluation of the document and previous plans (three-month evaluation supported by the Interamerican Foundation). Approval obtained to implement the forestry component of the strategy (ITTO–$222,000) and start of the first phase of this component.

1994   At the request of the Kuna people, the government declares 100,000 hectares as a reserve within the Comarca. Move to institutionalize PEMASKY as the Programme of Ecology and Management of Kuna-Yala Forest Areas.

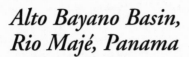

Alto Bayano Basin, Rio Majé, Panama

Sustainable Development Strategy

DIONISIO BATISTA, IUCN–PANAMA
WITH THE ASSISTANCE OF ARTURO LÓPEZ, IUCN

1 Introduction

The Alto Bayano, which covers an area of 350,000 hectares and is the largest hydro-electric basin in Panama, has been affected by colonization and deforestation since the 1970s. After 1976, the government tried to resolve the problems of land tenure and inefficient use of the land while trying to slow the pace of deforestation, but the conflicts continued to worsen with the passage of time. An official commission was set up in 1985 as a means of protecting the basin. Known as the Bayano Commission, it is composed of representatives of 11 national institutions, local communities and the private sector. In 1990, as part of the Tropical Forest Action Plan (TFAP), it was decided to start a regional strategy to guide the efforts of different institutions and help establish a framework of agreement between conflicting interests.

Little progress was made in the early years, apart from promoting the strategy within

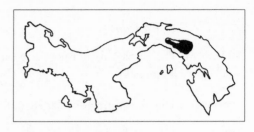

MAJÉ-BAYANO, PANAMA
Land area: 350,000 ha
Ecological zones: river basin, tropical forest
Main economic activities: timber and subsistence agriculture

the government itself and setting up the commission in 1990. Then in 1994 the change of government opened the way to more operational possibilities in the field. The difficult relations between indigenous people and peasants were finally improved when the groups reached an agreement halting further penetration of the forest. This was largely achieved through the introduction of proposals for economic alternatives, rather than by repressive policies. The alternatives put forward were aimed at solving the problems pointed out by the communities themselves.

Although the government is responsible for the strategy, there is no document formally setting out the new policies. It has attracted growing interest on the part of the government, however, which is now (1995) studying the possibility of expanding the strategy's application.

2 Scope and Objectives

The objective of the initial project was to protect the basin. The project has since evolved into a strategy with the following objectives:

- preserving the Alto Bayano basin, its ecological function and its water regulation capacity;
- sustainable development for local communities;
- preserving the characteristic biodiversity of the area;
- resolving inter-ethnic problems, particularly between indigenous groups and settlers; and
- regulating farming and forestry activities and offering the local population sustainable production alternatives.

3 Relationship to Development Planning

Although the government is responsible for the strategy, the latter has still not been formally set out in a document. The Bayano Commission has produced recommendations, however, which will constitute the basis of official policy for the area in the water, forest and conservation sectors. The TFAP and the activities of international aid organizations in this area have been fully integrated within these policies. It is possible that these policies will now be officially adopted. The government is showing a growing interest in incorporating the project with its policies and is considering the possibility of extending the area of the strategy to the whole of the basin.

4 Initial Development

Initially, the objective of the plan for managing the problems of the upper basin of the Bayano River was to protect the basin by stabilizing the advance of the agricultural frontier and by solving inter-ethnic problems. These were generating an escalating level of violence between indigenous groups (Kuna and Emberá) and settlers from the central provinces of Panama. After 1976, the government and other national organizations made an effort to resolve conflicts related to land use and tenure, and to halt the conversion of forests to other uses by cattle ranchers and loggers. The conflicts continued to worsen, however.

In 1985 the Bayano Commission was established. With the initiation of the TFAP in 1990, a management plan for the basin was prepared. This process began towards the end of 1993, with the financial support of Bundesministerium für Wirtschaftliche Zusammenarbeit (BMZ, Germany). IUCN provided technical assistance, and still plays an important role in promoting the actual strategy.

5   Implementation and Results

The establishment of the Bayano Commission constituted a real milestone, as did the incorporation of the TFAP in 1990. There were difficulties during the initiation phase, and because of having to start up the bureaucratic machinery before being able to move on to the field with a proposal. The government elected in 1994

supported the strategy and thus more progress with field work was achieved in a short period of time than had been accomplished previously.

Although strained relations between indigenous peoples and peasants affected the project considerably, in 1994 the opposing groups reached an agreement to stop invading the forest. This was achieved through the introduction of production alternatives aimed at solving the problems encountered by the communities, such as the security of food supplies. The basic tool was encouraging exchanges between the peasants. A further positive outcome was the fact that the Kuna-Bayano indigenous people, who had previously been reluctant to consider participating in government programmes, actually asked to participate in the project. This was the first time that this had happened in the community.

6   Lessons Learned

The limitations of the project include:

- colonization in indigenous Kuna and Emberá territories;
- invasion of Panama and political changes in 1989–1990, which held up the process and aggravated conflicts;
- poor support by the Ministry of Agriculture and other government bodies;

- limited participation by the communities in the early years; and
- lack of territorial planning or an overall strategy.

Among the opportunities realized were:

- emphasizing the basin's hydrological function as a national asset;
- integration of the strategy within the TFAP and links with international organizations; and
- the positive effects of the recent change of government.

The lessons learned include:

- working objectives must be politically viable;
- planning and coordination must be very dynamic and flexible, since conditions are variable and situations change;
- commitments with the communities must be dealt with effectively and expeditiously if credibility is to be preserved;
- work with the communities should begin by dealing with the priority problems brought up by the communities themselves, and peasants from other areas should be encouraged to exchange experiences.

7 Chronology

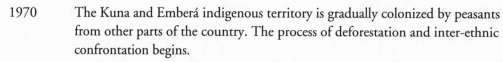

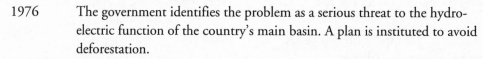

1970   The Kuna and Emberá indigenous territory is gradually colonized by peasants from other parts of the country. The process of deforestation and inter-ethnic confrontation begins.

1976   The government identifies the problem as a serious threat to the hydro-electric function of the country's main basin. A plan is instituted to avoid deforestation.

1985   Establishment of the Bayano Commission, composed of 11 representatives of national institutions, local communities and the private sector.

1986   CATIE undertakes a study of the situation in the basin.

1989   Invasion of Panama by the U S. Process halted for a year.

1990   Formulation of a Tropical Forest Action Plan for the area, with greater powers for the Commission, which is instructed to formulate a strategy for the whole of the basin.

1993   IUCN joins the Commission's work. Funds are obtained from BMZ for the implementation of the strategy.

1994   Initial contacts with the communities lead to agreements for the protection of the forest and the development of sustainable productive activities.

1995   The Kuna-Bayano people request participation in the process. The government considers extending the coverage area of the strategy.

Petén Region, Guatemala

Sustainable Development Strategy

Marco A Palacios M, SEGEPLAN
with the assistance of Alejandro C Imbach,
IUCN

1 Introduction

The Petén region, in the extreme north of
Guatemala between Mexico and Belize,
has a long history going back to the pre-
classical and classical periods of Mayan
culture. The territory contains some of the
Maya's finest works, such as the cities of
Tikal, Uaxactún, Yaxjá, Naranjo, Mirador
and others. The Maya left behind remarkable remains in the form of stone cities,
beautiful works of art, impressive engi-
neering achievements and the still unre-
solved mystery of their swift disappearance
at the end of the first millennium.

The tropical jungle invaded the inhabited
sites and engulfed the karstic plains and
hills that were the dominant feature in
Petén for hundreds of years. It was only in
this century that people returned in great
numbers to these warm lowlands. This
return has been linked to a number of
underlying structural problems in Guatemala, such as very high population density
on the Altiplano, concentration of land on
the south coast and degradation of natural

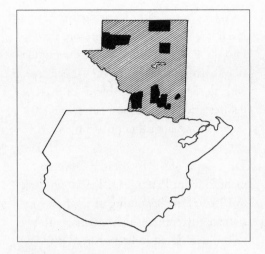

PETÉN REGION, GUATEMALA
Population: approximately 150,000
Land area: 3,600,000 ha
Ecological zones: flatlands, seasonal
tropical forest
Main economic activities: timber,
tourism, hunting

resources in the east. These factors have given rise to a powerful migratory flow into the Petén region, causing the population to grow at a rate of over 10 per cent, with all the resulting problems of massive deforestation, soil erosion, shortages of services for the local population, etc.

The origins of the Integrated Development Plan for Petén (PDI Petén) go back to 1987, at the beginning of the first civilian government in Guatemala after several decades of military rule. This civilian government took office under the mandate of a new National Constitution specifically mentioning the 'urgent economic integration of Petén' (transitional article No 15 of the Political Constitution of Guatemala) and undertook a regional assessment, which was completed in 1987 by the General Planning Department (SEGEPLAN).

At the same time as PDI Petén was launched, the government also established the National Environmental Commission (CONAMA). The government undertook this initiative as one of its immediate priorities to deal with the degradation of natural resources in Petén, and requested IUCN support to prepare a first regional sustainable development strategy for the area. This task was pursued jointly with CONAMA and SEGEPLAN during 1988, and the final document was used to negotiate a loan with the Federal Republic of Germany through the Kreditanstalt für

Wiederaufbau (KfW), with a view to preparing an integrated development plan setting out detailed guidelines for a development process in harmony with nature.

The plan was prepared between 1990 and 1992, under the coordination of the Planning Department's Petén Implementation Unit (UNEPET) and Agrar und Hydrotechnik (AHT), a German consultancy firm, with the participation of many national institutions and IUCN. As of 1995, the plan was still awaiting government approval.

2 Scope and Objectives

The Integrated Development Plan for Petén is a comprehensive proposal covering the whole of the Department of Petén (35,800 km^2). In conceptual terms, the Petén Plan explicitly adopts sustainable development as its basic goal, and covers all the main sectors of regional activity, such as:

- regulation of land tenure and use;
- social development;
- promotion of sustainable development among the communities;
- preservation of biological diversity (ecosystems, species and genes);
- energy and communications infrastructure;

- cattle farming, agroforestry and forestry activities;
- tourism;
- industrial activity and micro-enterprises; and
- institutional and legal aspects.

The specific objectives of the Integrated Development Plan are:

- to increase agricultural, stock-breeding and forestry productivity, while ensuring their sustainability;
- to protect the forest through a system of protected areas and the generation of alternative sources of income for the population;
- to apply and give effect to legislation protecting natural resources;
- to focus public action on improving services and the environmental situation;
- to regulate immigration according to the availability of suitable land;
- to protect the cultural and archaeological heritage;
- to develop an adequate communications network;
- to generate non-farm employment in Petén; and
- to develop adequate energy, drinking water and sanitation systems.

3 Relationship to National Institutions

UNEPET fully assumed its role as coordinator of national institutions (health, education, agriculture, forestry, protected areas, land, public works, etc), working with them to formulate the plan. In addition, through SEGEPLAN, the plan is coordinated with the country's development policies, which are less advanced in terms of adopting sustainability as their basic criterion, but not openly opposed to it.

The Integral Development Plan for Petén is not officially binding on the other ministries. However, a Petén Development Council has been established, with representation from all ministries. Implementing the plan is the mandate of this Council, which comprises nine representatives of ministries, 12 municipalities, two representatives from the private sector, two from workers groups, two from cooperatives and two from NGOs.

Petén has become the focus of action for some 30 NGOs of different kinds. They are coordinated and integrated by UNEPET through a specific NGO forum which meets regularly. The local communities have taken part in the planning process at regional level through their representatives (deputies, mayors and assistant mayors) and their own development organizations.

4 Initial Development

The Integrated Development Plan was prepared by SEGEPLAN through UNEPET, with technical assistance from Germany and other local, national, regional and international institutions.

It is worth mentioning that previous efforts, such as the Regional Strategy for the Sustainable Development of Petén (SEGEPLAN–CONAMA–IUCN), led to some sustainable rural development field projects in agricultural frontier areas of Petén. The projects included the Yaxjá Project (CONAP–IUCN), which began in 1990 and was financed successively by the Norwegian Agency for Development Cooperation (NORAD) and DANIDA; and the OLAFO–Petén (CONAP–CATIE) Project, financed by SIDA, NORAD and subsequently DANIDA, which was established in 1989.

These projects, which were developed on the same conceptual basis as the Integrated Development Plan, have not only provided a source of valuable experience for the implementation of plan projects, but have also proved to be a fund of valuable information, as in the case of the Proposal for the Integrated System of Protected Areas of Petén, prepared by CATIE–OLAFO and incorporated in the Plan.

5 Implementation and Results

Until the end of 1995, implementation work on the Integrated Development Plan was limited to using the resources of the national budget and external cooperation for the preparation of the plan, seeking government approval and obtaining funding for the Plan's new projects.

The implementation of some PDI projects has already begun. Some 70 per cent of the programmes and projects are currently at the stage of being negotiated with various governments (Germany, Taiwan, China, European Community) and with the Interamerican Development Bank and the World Bank. Projects currently being implemented include environmental improvement in central Petén, supplies of drinking water in Flores and in San Benito, a hydro-electric plant in El Camalote and some road development. At the same time, in view of the considerable number of national and foreign NGOs setting up their activities in Petén, UNEPET–SEGEPLAN VIII has undertaken to coordinate their activities systematically, using its legal powers of coordination and the PDI as a framework.

In this sense, most of these activities may be considered as those parts of the Petén Integrated Development Plan which are already being implemented. Many of them are concentrated in the Maya

Biosphere Reserve, which was set up in 1990 and which covers one third of the Petén region, encompassing an area of more than one million hectares. Some projects are run jointly with the National Council for Protected Areas (CONAP) for the management of the reserve, both in its core areas and in the buffer zones. The MAYARENA Project (CONAP-USAID) assists CONAP in supervising and monitoring the reserve and runs a broad-ranging environmental education programme in the buffer zone.

Other projects were started before the Biosphere Reserve was established (OLAFO–Petén, 1989; and Yaxjá, 1990) in the agricultural frontier areas. When the reserve was set up, they found themselves located inside it. Both projects work actively with the local communities, with the objective of stabilizing the agricultural frontier by improving peasant farming systems and by introducing new alternatives, based on the comprehensive and sustained use of forest resources (timber and non-timber) and on local processing of those resources (handicrafts, woodwork, etc). While the Yaxjá project is focused more on rural development, the Conservation for Sustainable Development Project in Central America (OLAFO) concentrates on studying the management of resources, so that their efforts are complementary and they are able to develop more comprehensive activities within their respective areas.

6 Lessons Learned

The preparation and implementation of the PDI for Petén has yielded a considerable store of experience, which may be summarized as follows:

- it is possible to adopt a regional sustainable development concept and to incorporate it officially within a broader plan which covers not only conservation but also more traditional development aspects (such as production, communications, services, etc);
- the government body in charge of the process has assumed a coordinating role, linking the implementation efforts of both governmental and non-governmental bodies within a coherent scheme;
- the political instability inherent in most Latin American governments caused a series of delays in the process, but did not stop it altogether, thanks to the written undertakings obtained from the government in support of the institutions involved, and to the persistence of the working group responsible for the continuity of the process;
- a broad level of participation was achieved, even though generally speaking the communities only participated through their local political representatives (mayors, deputy mayors, etc). One lesson learned was to avoid going to the communities at election time;

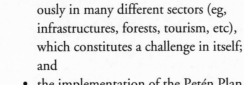
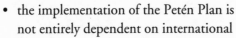

- actions must be initiated simultaneously in many different sectors (eg, infrastructures, forests, tourism, etc), which constitutes a challenge in itself; and
- the implementation of the Petén Plan is not entirely dependent on international support, since many of its activities are part of the work plans of national institutions which coordinate the preparation of its budgets and the implementation of its activities through SEGEPLAN–UNEPET.

7   Chronology

AD 900   Highest point of the classical period of Mayan culture in Petén.

1000   Emigration of last Mayan groups to other regions.

1900   Beginning of extractive activity for the production of gum, peppers and timber in Petén.

1959   Establishment of the FYDEP (Promotion and Development of Petén), the first body responsible for the region's development. FYDEP was autonomous and carried full responsibility for all activities in the region. It constituted an insurmountable obstacle to the entry of any other governmental institutions in the territory.

1985   Election of the civilian government of Dr Vinicio Cerezo A.

1987   SEGEPLAN completes the regional diagnosis for Petén.

1988   SEGEPLAN–CONAMA–IUCN prepare the sustainable development strategy for Petén.

1989   SEGEPLAN comes to Petén and sets up the Implementation Unit of the Integrated Development Plan for Petén (UNEPET), initiating the process of inter-institutional and inter-sectoral coordination.

1990   Creation of the Maya Biosphere Reserve.

1990–92   SEGEPLAN–UNEPET and AHT head the preparation of the Integrated Development Plan for Petén, and the PROSELVA Programme for the Protection of the Tropical Forest.

1992–94   Establishment of the Petén Information Centre and construction of two buildings for the sub-regional offices of SEGEPLAN in Sayaxché and Poptún.

1992–94   SEGEPLAN joins the Advisory Council of the Maya Biosphere Reserve and the Mayan Technical Council. A land survey is launched, together with a procedure for the legalization of land holdings in buffer zones.

1994   Institution of the NGO Monthly Forum.

Plains of Tortuguero, Costa Rica

Sustainable Development Strategy

LUIS A ROJAS, MIRENEM
JAVIER JIMENEZ AND ARTURO LÓPEZ, PACTO
WITH THE ASSISTANCE OF ROBERT PRESCOTT-ALLEN, IUCN–CESP

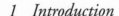

1 Introduction

The formulation of the Strategy for the Plains of Tortuguero (Costa Rica) started at the end of 1990 with an agreement between the Ministry for Natural Resources (MIRENEM), the European Economic Community (EEC) and IUCN. Joint biophysical, socio-economic and legal studies were undertaken, and in 1991 a draft strategy was produced, which was revised and endorsed for the Ministry by 80 organizations. The formulation process attracted the participation of central government departments, municipal leaders, producer associations, NGOs, local organizations and a solid technical team.

In 1991, the strategy's initial objective was to establish the Tortuguero Conservation Area (ACTo), on the basis of a zoning plan covering 170,000 hectares of land, which would be subject to certain ecologi-

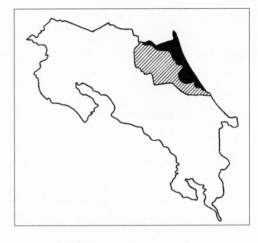

TORTUGUERO, COSTA RICA
Population: 140,000
Land area: 514,000 ha
Ecological zones: coastal flatlands, tropical rainforest
Main economic activities: bananas, tourism, cattle, timber

cal, socio-economic and cultural constraints. The conservation area consists of a core zone of 75,000 hectares, the priority for which was the conservation of biodiversity, and a buffer or multiple-use zone of 95,000 hectares, providing incentives and support for the sustainable development of the local population. The strategy also suggests guidelines for the sustainable development of a surrounding area of influence covering up to 419,000 hectares, and includes a self-financing plan to ensure sustainability.

After 1992 no further effort was made in the communities to work on a general planning basis or to insist on a regional strategy. Instead, communal strategies were initiated in six critical communities either on the coast or on the agricultural frontier, and a series of projects was launched. Some of the projects were earmarked for the communities, some for technical and administrative support; one set up communal banks to deal with the financial aspects of the projects. Agreements were signed for the implementation of activities, at first with producer associations, and later directly with the communities. Assistance was provided to set up local tourism and fishing facilities. As part of the land-use planning programme, a participatory survey of population, land use and ownership was carried out in order to establish land tenure guarantees for local inhabitants.

The strategy was partially held up in the middle of 1993 owing to delays in the financing of the subsequent phase. Although this period caused problems for the technical team, it did provide an opportunity to strengthen the internal organization of the Project for the Consolidation of the Tortuguero Conservation Area (PACTo), and to establish priorities and optimize the implementation phase, as well as obtain further support from national sources, particularly the Ministry for Natural Resources.

Draft legislation in February 1994 established the Conservation Area, which covered a total of 176,100 hectares of land (with fewer than 15,000 inhabitants). In February 1995 a major area of influence covering up to 514,000 hectares (with 140,000 inhabitants) was added.

The strategy has yielded a great deal of experience and many lessons. One of these is that all participants, including the government and donors, must understand that a sustainable development strategy is a long-term process, and not just a one-time funding exercise. It is also important to strengthen local and national capacity for sustainable development throughout the process by delegating responsibilities and making good use of existing capacity. Another lesson is the benefit derived from having full community participation from the beginning, without relying solely on

local leaders. Communities are better represented by sectors that they organize for themselves, such as health, sport, development, or education. It was only after an initial period of discussions on sustainable development planning, through a participatory diagnosis of problems and solutions, environmental education, and the provision of seed funds to support local initiatives, that the support of the communities was secured and the necessary degree of credibility was achieved.

The Main Issues

Costa Rica has a remarkable system of protected natural areas that cover 11.2 per cent of the country; however, the protection of biodiversity is not guaranteed outside these areas. In 1992, the country's rate of deforestation was the highest in Latin America, and it is estimated that tropical rainforest suitable for logging will be exhausted by the year 2010. Protected areas are being isolated one from the other; some are threatened by pollution from external sources. People living near the protected areas often consider them obstacles to economic development. With population growth and immigration, the agricultural frontier is constantly advancing, bringing strong pressure to bear on these areas.

The Tortuguero National Park (PNT), with 18,946 hectares on land and 52,000 hectares at sea; and the Barra del Colorado Forest Wildlife Refuge (RBC), at 92,000 hectares, were set up in 1972 and 1985 respectively. The two areas were subsequently physically and administratively merged into ACTo, which constitutes Costa Rica's main contribution to the Integrated System of Protected Areas for Peace (SIAPAZ) programme run jointly with Nicaragua. The PNT remains national property and is under full protection, although the surrounding area has an annual deforestation rate of ten per cent per year. The RBC was set up on private property and is located in a typical agricultural frontier, with an annual deforestation rate of four per cent (representing 3,500 hectares per year) between 1984 and 1991.

In April 1990, in order to physically unite the conservation area and the refuge, the government set up the Tortuguero Protected Zone on land mainly suited to forestry or conservation. Local peasants and the logging company operating there attacked the government's action as unconstitutional. Although the state was buying properties with funds donated by NGOs, some property owners were unwilling to sell, and the land purchases gave rise to new invasions. Land reclamation reached as far as the edge of the coastal marshes, where individuals who had sold land to the 'biological corridor' invaded and claimed areas of land in the marshes with the intention of 'selling' them back to the conservationists.

Efforts to pass legislation creating buffer zones around the protected areas made little progress until 1995, owing to the fact that the Costa Rican constitution establishes the private right to define the use of land on private property. By 1995, environmental guarantees had been built into the constitution, allowing a certain control over activities outside state properties.

ACTo now has 140,000 inhabitants, although less than 15,000 of them live in the buffer zone, and less than 500 live in the core zone. In the buffer zone, the population is split into 20 communities, consisting of two main cultures: Creole peasants in the interior and on the banks of rivers and lakes, and mainly Afro-Caribbean fishermen on the coast.

The coastal communities felt confined between the sea on one side and the protected areas on the other. This was the case until 1992, when their participation in the strategy became more substantial. Meanwhile, the communities in the interior felt trapped between the protected areas and the advance of monoculture banana plantations, which more than doubled in area between 1984 and 1992 (from 21,000 to 44,000 hectares).

Other problems arose from deforestation: erosion; pollution generated by banana companies; lack of fishing regulations throughout the area; lack of land tenure guarantees (affecting over 70 per cent of the population in the buffer zone); and lack of credit for sustainable productive activities. Government assistance is generally limited throughout the area to the National Park and Forest Wildlife Services (responsible for the park and reserve respectively).

2 Objectives and Focus

The strategy's focus is sustainable development, and it has the following objectives:

- maintaining ecosystems and biodiversity, and demonstrating that socio-economic development is the best guarantee of conservation;
- reforming current development policies in the region;
- land-use planning and the establishment of a 514,000-hectare conservation area, consisting of a core zone (to act as a biological corridor between Costa Rica and Nicaragua), a buffer zone and a zone of influence;
- generating wide-ranging discussion concerning the significance and implications of sustainable development, and coordinating joint actions between the government and various social and economic sectors; and
- strengthening the capacity of local communities for self-diagnosis, organization and environmentally sustainable socio-economic development.

3 Relationship to Development Planning

MIRENEM and the Ports and Atlantic Development Board of Administration (JAPDEVA) have both given their support to the strategy. Together with the Ministry of Planning (MIDEPLAN) and the Institute for Agrarian Development (IDA), they participated in the preparation of the initial document until 1992.

ACTo was set up by decree in 1994. From an institutional point of view, ACTo coordinates three previously separate general directorates: forestry, forest wildlife and national parks. In practice, ACTo also coordinates the actions of NGOs working in the area and acts as a link with international cooperation programmes. In the near future it is hoped that a regional committee will be set up, with the participation of the Ministries of Agriculture and Stock-breeding and Rural Development, the main producer organizations and NGOs.

The strategy, although still not official, had a decisive effect on the legal establishment of the conservation area, and has influenced the implementation of sectoral plans, such as the Forest Action Plans. It has also affected formal education and the regulation of the expansion of banana plantations, while helping to establish priorities and generate coordination between various international donor agencies.

4 Initial Development and Organization

The strategy began with the signing of an agreement between the Government of Costa Rica, acting through MIRENEM, and the EEC. Its implementation was launched in October 1990. The project, known as PACTo, was run jointly until 1992 by the MIRENEM and the IUCN Regional Office for Central America (IUCN–ORCA).

A team of eight technicians, taken from different institutions and with different specializations, was coordinated by the joint managers of PACTo (MIRENEM and the EEC). The team enlisted as many as 100 organizations, including government institutions, producer groups, NGOs, companies, academic departments and communal development associations with an interest in the conservation and socio-economic development of the Plains of Tortuguero. Approximately 12 to 15 organizations were most involved, and were able to strike a balance between their socio-economic backgrounds and their interest in conservation and/or development. Tasks were distributed among them, until a team of 24 technicians was set up, with a further 13 auxiliary or part-time members.

Initially the technical team was divided into four working groups – biophysical, socio-economic, institutional and legal –

with one local peasant team. The team collated existing information which, though abundant, was dispersed among many institutions. Team members also carried out field surveys and investigations, generated new information wherever necessary and took advantage of the process as an opportunity to attract the participation of new partners.

The next phase (lasting four months) consisted of a joint analysis of information through six sectoral workshops and plenaries, consultation meetings and visits to the communities. At the same time, the information was used to produce maps on different themes, while the public were informed through pamphlets and short radio programmes. Local teachers were also enlisted to help prepare an environmental education strategy for the area. In subsequent workshops, which were attended by representatives of up to 80 different organizations, priority problems were identified and causes and effects were analyzed from an inter-sectoral point of view. As a result of this work, an additional workshop was able to establish action priorities and working guidelines. For instance, the area was subdivided into 23 sub-areas, following a classification of human communities, based on 15 biophysical and 15 socio-economic variables in each sub-area. This led to the identification of those critical areas (combining maximum biodiversity with minimum

socio-economic potential) where the strategy should concentrate its efforts.

The following phase, lasting six months, saw the formulation and revision of the first draft of the strategy. The Small Producers' Association (UPAGRA), with 3,000 members in the area, and the Loggers Association (ASIREA) made detailed revisions to the first draft. Meanwhile, field projects were started in the sectors of forest management, agricultural diversification and organizational training, among others.

A second draft of the document was prepared and widely circulated among participants. Preliminary draft legislation was also prepared, which included the establishment of the conservation area. Contributions were made by producer organizations (UPAGRA and Justice and Development), although they proved reluctant to envisage any sort of legal limitation on socio-economic conditions prevailing in the buffer zone. The framework for actions is provided by a land-use plan, which includes a revised, updated version of the land survey, and which aims to settle land tenure conflicts by giving guarantees of ownership to the local inhabitants.

Part of the process was held up in the middle of 1993 owing to delays in the funding of the subsequent phase. Al-

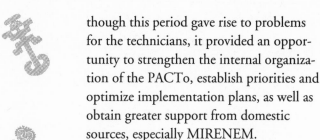

though this period gave rise to problems for the technicians, it provided an opportunity to strengthen the internal organization of the PACTo, establish priorities and optimize implementation plans, as well as obtain greater support from domestic sources, especially MIRENEM.

After 1992, the process changed. Less emphasis was placed on overall planning and the participation of broad regional and national sectors. Instead, the focus was field work with the communities. In the target groups, there was no further insistence on introducing a regional strategy. Instead, community strategies were initiated in the six critical communities (three on the coast and three on the agricultural frontier). Implementation began on projects identified by the communities as being part of their own strategies, with the provision of technical and administrative assistance and the creation of communal banks to manage project funding. Agreements were signed for the implementation of activities, initially with the above-mentioned producers' associations, and then directly with the communities.

Despite the significant progress achieved so far, the links within the strategy are still somewhat tentative. The field projects and communal strategies may help the communities and organizations involved to become more aware of the importance of sustainable development to the region as a whole, and to the overall Tortuguero strategy. On the other hand, they might lead to a weakening of the overall process, or to the general strategy disintegrating into a series of independent projects and communal strategies.

5 Implementation and Results

The technical team had to overcome powerful mistrust of the conservation projects among people in the communities, who expressed particular antipathy for MIRENEM, JAPDEVA and other state institutions. After 18 months, during which the participatory process matured, the parties involved arrived at a general consensus concerning the need for a significant change in conservation and development policies. They initially focused on the creation of a new conservation area. The extent of consensus on other aspects of the strategy is less clear. What is definite is that both conservation and long-term planning were given a hearing by the communities, although only to the extent that they were combined with socio-economic improvements.

Land-use planning: Local inhabitants participated in a population census. It yielded data on land tenure, the state of properties and their production. The data was then used as a basis for attributing plots and land titles in the most disputed areas.

Forest resources: ACTo has helped the local population obtain information and take advantage of existing financial and technical incentives. Schemes have been launched to promote the establishment and management of communal forests in two communities, while two additional pilot forest projects have been supported in recently legalized estates. A total of 75 forestry permits have been issued in the area, following another series of forestry management plans implemented for the estates. A review is currently underway of the extent to which these plans have actually been put into effect by the beneficiaries.

Aquatic resources: Work has been centred on the Barra del Colorado community, leading to the establishment of the first fishermen's association in the region, providing assistance to fishermen without equipment, and setting up a community bank. In Barra de Tortuguero, the second largest coastal settlement, an ecotourism programme provided a course for local guides.

Environmental education: Many workshops were held with the 70 teachers of the area. Videos, audiovisual material and radio programmes were produced. The Ministry of Education has recognized the course given to teachers as being part of the official curriculum. Teachers who have attended the course receive a monthly allowance of US$10. Formal and informal environmental education activities have significantly increased local support for the conservation area and have helped to start up activities in remote communities.

Banana plantations: In the early part of 1992, IUCN carried out an assessment of the environmental impact of the expansion of banana plantations in the Atlantic region of Costa Rica (Sarapiquí, Tortuguero and Talamanca), recommending guidelines to minimize their ecological and socio-economic impact. Although these guidelines have not yet been applied, a verbal commitment was obtained from the banana multinationals by MIRENEM halting the expansion of further cultivation within the conservation area. This commitment has so far been fulfilled, thanks no doubt in part to the removal, in 1992, of European banana import quotas.

Other projects: Field projects with the communities have been strengthened, including the attribution of land title, communal diagnoses, communal sustainable development plans, agricultural/forestry/pastoral systems, small-scale fishing, waste management, renewable energy, transport and drinking water. Agreements for the implementation of the projects have been signed with the communities, and are revised and renewed every three months.

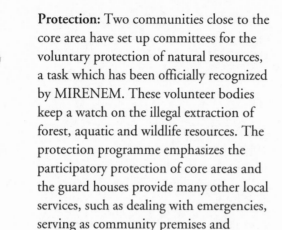

Protection: Two communities close to the core area have set up committees for the voluntary protection of natural resources, a task which has been officially recognized by MIRENEM. These volunteer bodies keep a watch on the illegal extraction of forest, aquatic and wildlife resources. The protection programme emphasizes the participatory protection of core areas and the guard houses provide many other local services, such as dealing with emergencies, serving as community premises and organizing environmental education.

Financial support and training: The ACTo strategy has supported local initiatives with seed funds. UPAGRA, for instance, received US$50,000 to train small farmers to administer projects, and to help them develop ecotourism and forest management projects. Training is also provided for production and for services. Communal banks have been set up to finance these activities using rotating funds. Although the strategy is dependent on external funds (mainly from the European Union) for field projects, it has a growing component of national financing. This currently funds 70 per cent of the official staff involved and is sure to increase in the future.

Coordination: There is coordination among the sectors of fisheries, tourism, natural resources, energy, health, drinking water and public security. Although there is no formal coordinating committee, a

monitoring committee meets every three months, with the participation of the three general directorates of MIRENEM (forestry, forest wildlife and national parks). These will soon be joined by the energy department, in addition to the donor (the EEC) and IUCN. The strategy also coordinates the activities of NGOs working in the area.

Community Strategies

In the beginning, participation was to some extent informal; that is, individuals from the various organizations were not always official representatives with the power to undertake commitments. Neither was there any clear procedure by which they could obtain a commitment on the part of their organizations. During most of the formulation process, the communities participated through their leaders, and their participation did not increase until the communal strategies were launched.

The priority populations began to assess their own problems. In Tortuguero, for instance, the issues included public transport and tourism managed by the community. In Barra del Colorado, discussions centred on the management of fisheries, organization for production and marketing, roll-over credits, land-use planning, and the establishment of a communal forest. In Pueblo Nuevo, the focus was on environmental education, nature trails, analysis and supply of water and the protection of aquifers. In Palacios and Linda Vista, the important issue was the sustainable management of the forest in selected estates.

Communal strategies were formulated by the technical team and by members of each community. The team began by identifying key individuals in each community to initiate discussions about local problems and requirements, and about sustainable development as an alternative to conventional development. At the same time environmental education programmes were introduced in schools, seed funds were provided for local initiatives, and training courses were given in organization and production. The next step was to initiate a cooperative relationship with other local organizations by learning about their programmes and experience, analyzing their points of view about local problems, and seeking appropriate coordination mechanisms.

Communal strategies were initially coordinated by the governing boards of local development associations. These associations were made up of the residents of the communities. Later, a substantial improvement was introduced in the form of 'councils of notables', which brought together communal representatives not only on matters of development, but also health, sport, education and other sectors

recognized by the community. These councils turned out to be significantly more representative than the development associations. Representatives of the six councils of notables already established meet every six months to coordinate their work and exchange experience.

6 Lessons Learned

Main factors against the strategy include:

- structural adjustment programmes and the priority allocation of credit and technical support for non-sustainable production activities;
- land speculation and the rapid displacement of peasants as a result of the expansion of banana plantations;
- the limited control exercised by institutions on the development of their own and other programmes when making use of natural resources;
- the precarious social conditions of many communities in the area, the lack of an organizational basis in the handling of natural resources, and the lack of guarantees for land tenure;
- the initial hostility of communities towards protected natural areas as a result of the state of social abandonment in which the government had left them, and of initial pressures by some conservationist sectors to buy land and to expand the national park without

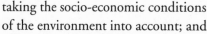

taking the socio-economic conditions of the environment into account; and

- the duplication and lack of coordination in relations between institutions and NGOs, and the distrust of a process run by a single ministry.

Main factors in favour of the strategy were:

- the work done by ECODES made organizations and area leaders aware of the concept and the importance of sustainable development;
- the understanding, unconditional support and clarity of the governing bodies of MIRENEM and the donor in overcoming the project's difficulties and conflicts;
- participants were actually brought closer together by some structural problems, such as the socio-environmental effects of the expansion of banana plantations; and
- the favourable results likely to occur with the declaration of sustainable development as the central policy of the Government of Costa Rica (1994-98).

Main Lessons Learned

From the point of view of strategy formulation, lessons included:

- the formulation of a sub-national strategy is not a document but a process

of analysis, consensus, training and change in attitudes, behaviour and practice;

- there is no single recipe for content, even at the community level, although it is possible to identify some methodological guidelines;
- the active participation of all sectors involved in conservation and development is an essential requirement of the process. Participation is much more than consultation and should take the form of shared responsibility;
- all existing information must be made use of in order to represent all viewpoints and to generate participation from the outset;
- the project must act as a catalyst, a guide and a supervisor of the process; it must take advantage of and strengthen existing capacity in the region so that the process can be continued by national or local players once the sponsoring project has been completed;
- it is important to maintain an interdisciplinary – if possible an interinstitutional – promoting team, and to involve intermediate-level officials as well as senior officials in decisionmaking; in addition, technical staff should be national citizens;
- it is important to have a clear commitment on the part of the government in favour of any changes or processes, and to have close coordination between donor, government and implementing agency;

- budgets should be adequate and flexible to cover the cost of workshops, exchanges, small publications and seed funds; and
- it is preferable to take action without spending too much time on exhaustive planning.

From the point of view of application in the field, lessons include:

- there was a need to implement local strategies in communities which were most representative of different development styles and traditions;
- priority should be given to aspects which the communities themselves have identified as urgent, even when they do not concern natural resources;
- a closer and more direct contact has to be sought directly with the communities, not only through their leaders;
- it is worth promoting committees which include all the community's representative bodies, not just official or traditional institutions; and
- communal banks based on a savings and loan system should be established for the implementation of projects.

7 Chronology

1972 Establishment of the Tortuguero National Park.

1972 Establishment of the Forest Wildlife Refuge of Barra del Colorado.

1988 Costa Rica and Nicaragua sign the SIAPAZ frontier agreement.

1990 In October, MIRENEM, EEC and IUCN initiate the Project for the Consolidation of the Tortuguero Conservation Area (PACTo).

1991 January–February: establishment of technical strategy coordination with the participation of MIRENEM, JAPDEVA AND IUCN. Initiation of discussions concerning the concept and methodology of the strategy with a team of peasant leaders and representatives of the main NGOs.

March–May: team expanded to 24 technicians belonging to various institutions and groups carries out basic studies, and environmental education strategy begins to be applied.

June–September: up to 80 representatives of different organizations in six sectoral and plenary workshops analyze available information and draw up the first draft of the strategy.

October: a three-day plenary workshop revises the draft of the strategy and sends MIRENEM a declaration expressing its support for the strategy and its concern at the conflict between the strategy and the rapid expansion of banana plantations.

1992 January-February: the draft of the strategy is reviewed by communal leaders and production sectors, who submit their comments for a second draft; IUCN carries out the Environmental Impact Assessment (EIA) into the effects of the monoculture of bananas and a commitment is obtained from the multinationals to halt expansion in the area.

March–May: the second draft of the strategy is proposed in consultation with communal leaders and producer associations; guidelines are established for the management of the core zone and preliminary draft legislation is tabled before the Legislative Assembly for the sustainable development of the Plains of Tortuguero.

May–October: a participatory survey is initiated in ACTo, at the same time as two communal strategies and pilot projects in three priority communities; strategy agreements with UPAGRA and with development associations of Tortuguero and Pueblo Nuevo.

1993   PACTo arrives at a 'bridging' stage, almost devoid of external finance for eight months; MIRENEM commits a growing percentage of national funding, covering up to 70 per cent of the officials involved. The strategy is focused on community priorities, and agreements are signed with an additional three critical communities. Field projects with the communities are consolidated through the issue of land titles, communal diagnoses, communal sustainable development plans and combined agricultural/forestry/pastoral schemes.

1994   February: ACTo (core zone and buffer zone) is set up by decree with 171,000 hectares; its governing body coordinates the three previously separate general directorates: forestry, forest wildlife and national parks.

May: the new government (1994–1998) adopts sustainable development as a policy guideline for the legislature and submits a programme of practical measures. 'Councils of notables' are set up in the six priority communities, with communal representatives of the development, health, sport, education and other sectors recognized by the community; representatives of the six councils of notables meet every three months to coordinate activities and compare experience. Communal banks are set up to finance activities, using roll-over funds; projects include small-scale fishing, waste management, renewable energy, transport and drinking water.

1995   February: a new decree extends the conservation area to the entire 514,000-hectare area considered in the 1992 proposal by adding an area of influence of 340,000 hectares. Volunteer groups are set up at the request of some communities for the protection of natural resources, including forests, fishing and wildlife. Permanent coordination is set up among the sectors of fishing, tourism, natural resources, energy, health, drinking water and public safety.

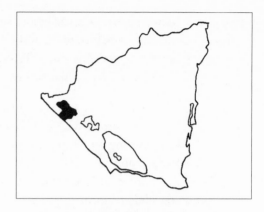

Héroes y Mártires de Veracruz and Pikin-Guerrero, Nicaragua

Management Plan and Sustainable Development Project

ALAIN MEYRAT, IUCN–PÍKIN
VICTOR CEDEÑO, IUCN–NICARAGUA
WITH THE ASSISTANCE OF ALEJANDRO C IMBACH,
IUCN–CESP

1   Introduction and Summary

The Héroes y Mártires de Veracruz management plan covers an area of over 200,000 hectares in the areas of Léon and Chinandega in northwest Nicaragua. The area includes the volcanic mountain range of Los Maribios and its foothills and coastal plain, which contains the country's best agricultural land.

The area is now very much degraded due to the extensive monoculture of cotton. This has completely denuded the plain and generated a devastating process of deforestation. It has also displaced the small-holding peasants to the foothills of the mountains and the coastal mangroves, polluted the environment with massive quantities of pesticides, and depleted the productive capacity of the natural resource base. Water and wind erosion of the soils have followed, along with periodic floods,

HÉROES y MÁRTIRES, NICARAGUA
Population: approximately 50,000;
Pikin 20,000
Land area: 200,000 ha; Pikin 43,600 ha
Ecological zones: volcanic slopes and coastal flatlands
Main economic activities: cotton, coffee, agriculture

which have destroyed bridges, roads, railways and infrastructure.

The Héroes y Mártires de Veracruz management plan was jointly designed by the Institute for Natural Resources and the Environment (IRENA) and IUCN in 1986–1987, and was later implemented through a series of specific field projects dealing with different aspects of the region's problems. One of these projects is Pikin-Guerrero, which is one of the case studies considered in this chapter.

Although the projects are currently in the process of being implemented, the management plan's central coordination and conceptual cohesion have decreased over the years. The overall objectives of the plan have been lost, along with the possibility of reviving it as a strategic tool for the environmental recovery of this key area.

Like other regional and national strategies, it served in its time to introduce conservation objectives into development plans, to provide a basis for reflection on regional development, to initiate some coordinated priority actions and to provide a framework for programmes which had already been started with external cooperation.

The Pikin-Guerrero project, which includes training and roll-over credits, benefits 700 families of farmers and 300 families of loggers in the middle and lower reaches of the basin, over a total area of 15,000 hectares. The project is now entering its third phase, where the emphasis is on land-use planning – to provide protection for forests and biodiversity in the upper basin – for an area of 43,600 hectares. The experience gained with this project has been considerable, both in terms of improving the local population's social and working conditions and of preserving biodiversity.

2 Scope and Objectives

The management plan was essentially aimed at the recovery and conservation of natural resources (soils, water, forests, forest wildlife) as the basis for a gradual sustainable improvement in the living conditions of the local population. Its objectives were:

- to consolidate the protected areas established by the IRENA Institute (now MARENA, the Ministry for the Environment and Natural Resources) in the highlands of Los Maribios and in coastal mangroves;
- to recover the ecological functions of ecosystems on the mountain slopes of Los Maribios, working in conjunction with peasant cooperatives;
- to develop alternative sustainable forms of production for coastal mangroves;
- to control erosion in the plain, restore the area's fertility and change its use to

more appropriate production activities than cotton monoculture; and

- to manage the area comprehensively so as to coordinate all actions undertaken in the upper, middle and lower parts of the various basins within a unified scheme.

3 Relationship to National Institutions

The management plan was prepared by the Department of Protected Areas and Forest Fauna of IRENA, with the technical assistance of IUCN consultants, and the initial field projects (Pikín Guerrero, Los Maribios and OLAFO–mangroves) were jointly prepared by the institutions concerned and IRENA.

The regional directorate of IRENA–Region II was at first in charge of the overall coordination of the management plan. This arrangement underwent a considerable number of changes in the following six years, until IRENA was replaced by MARENA.

The field projects obtained the backing of many governmental and non-governmental institutions. For example, Pikín Guerrero was supported by the Autonomous University of Nicaragua (based in Léon), the National Union of Farmers and Stockbreeders, the Municipalities of Chichigalpa and Posoltega, the Nicara-

guan Environmentalist Movement and others, which have been actively involved in field work with the peasants and their cooperatives.

4 Initial Development

The initial stage of the plan consisted of identifying regional and international institutions, such as IUCN, the Agroeconomic Research and Education Centre (CATIE) and the United Nations Food and Agriculture Organization (FAO), which might be interested in developing activities in the area. It also involved preparing proposals for specific projects and seeking international financial support to implement them. Three field projects were launched as a result.

a. The Pikín Guerrero project was developed jointly by IRENA and IUCN, with NORAD funding. The project is located in the northern part of Héroes y Mártires, on the slopes of the San Cristóbal-Casita volcanic chain. It was launched in 1988 and went through two stages as a joint IUCN–IRENA project before being fully taken over by IRENA in 1993. The project covers a broad range of activities related to the production and conservation of natural resources. It originally covered an area of some 15,000 hectares with 15,000 inhabitants, and has now been extended to 47,000 hectares with 20,000 inhabitants.

b. The development project of Los Maribios was developed jointly by FAO and IRENA, with Netherlands funding. This project began in 1989 in a location similar to that of the Pikín Guerrero project, but to the extreme south, near the town of Léon. Its objectives are similar to those of Pikín Guerrero, but the methodology is based on rural development with model farms. The project is still being run by the original institutions at the time of writing (1995).

c. The OLAFO–Manglares project was developed jointly by IRENA and CATIE through the Project for Conservation and Development in Central America. It was financed in its first phase by SIDA and NORAD, with the added cooperation of DANIDA in the second phase. This project is located in the mangrove area of Héroes y Mártires and is an attempt to establish systems of sustainable production in the mangroves, such as processing to extract charcoal and tannin, along with other activities, including sea and estuary fishing.

In the last two years, there have been other initiatives that would fit within the conceptual framework of Héroes y Mártires, such as the Cortinas Forestales project (IRENA–FINNIDA). Unfortunately, because formal coordination for Héroes y Mártires has been abandoned in practice by default, and because the scheme has not been officially declared by the Ministry as part of its policy for the region, it is doubtful whether these other initiatives will ever become part of Héroes y Mártires. Despite this, there is a continuity of approach.

5 Implementation and Results

Both the Pikín Guerrero and the OLAFO projects are community-based. The groups are organized in different ways and carry out activities which they consider most appropriate to local circumstances. The Maribios project is more oriented to working with model farms, where peasants can learn how to continue the proposed activities.

OLAFO–Manglares began with a detailed survey of the land and sea flora and fauna resources in the mangrove area. This was followed by discussions with the communities to determine appropriate ways of using these resources, to ensure that the intensity of extraction did not exceed the rate of regeneration. In view of the population density in these areas, a number of activities have been started with a view to increasing local processing of resources (such as charcoal, tannin, salt, handicrafts based on local produce, etc), in order to generate additional income and thereby reduce pressure on the mangroves.

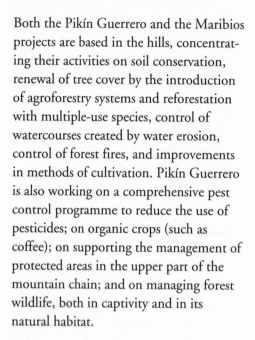

Both the Pikín Guerrero and the Maribios projects are based in the hills, concentrating their activities on soil conservation, renewal of tree cover by the introduction of agroforestry systems and reforestation with multiple-use species, control of watercourses created by water erosion, control of forest fires, and improvements in methods of cultivation. Pikín Guerrero is also working on a comprehensive pest control programme to reduce the use of pesticides; on organic crops (such as coffee); on supporting the management of protected areas in the upper part of the mountain chain; and on managing forest wildlife, both in captivity and in its natural habitat.

The results achieved by the Pikín Guerrero project are:

- training of agricultural technicians, who in turn will train local farmers, who then act as local promoters for farm planning, production and marketing;
- agroforestry promotion, including training for farm planning, soil and water conservation, agricultural diversification, comprehensive pest control, nurseries, plantations, and incorporating women in the production process (this has been particularly successful – 82 women have been trained);
- forest protection and management and training in forest inventories and management (each year, public cam-

paigns in the countryside teach people fire control, reducing the frequency of fire outbreaks by half and of burnt areas by 75 per cent in just three years;
- environmental education and health, with the participation of 200 teachers in charge of 4,000 children in the area. The project supports the Ministry of Health in providing primary health care to 6,000 community dwellers, and sex education has also been provided for adults; and
- irrational logging has been reduced, production systems have become more stable from an economic point of view, and the net income of families taking part in the project has been improved.

These three projects have gained valuable and varied experience. Unfortunately, because of the disbanding of the overall coordinating authority for the Héroes y Mártires scheme, this experience has not been exchanged, systematized or disseminated. On the basis of the progress made so far, including the degree of credibility achieved, the project is currently (1995) advocating restarting a sustainable development strategy for the region.

6 Lessons Learned

The Héroes y Mártires de Veracruz Project, as an overall process, has produced some interesting lessons:

- the grave crisis in production and the destruction of expensive infrastructure works (roads, bridges, etc) had the effect of triggering the preparation of the management plan, reconfirming the human tendency to react rather than to anticipate and prevent;
- environmental questions only became really important when they affected aspects of traditional economies, which highlights the very limited penetration achieved by sustainability concepts in some government bodies;
- there is a need for a permanent mechanism for follow-up work on projects implemented within the broad conceptual framework of the strategy. This follow-up work should be carried out by government agencies;
- there is a need for specific field activities to test strategic guidelines in practice in order to enrich the general framework of the scheme and to enable it to evolve and to gain in-depth experience. In the case of the Héroes y Mártires project, these feedback mechanisms never materialized;
- the involvement of both government and civilian institutions and sectors in field projects was and is crucial for their success, especially when projects enter stages of institutional transfer, as in the case of Pikín Guerrero; and

- the projects were very instructive for technicians, inhabitants and participating institutions alike. Nevertheless, few of the lessons were disseminated to other sectors (government, other peasants, conservation and development institutions, etc).

The analysis of the Píkin Guerrero project in particular also highlights many lessons:

- the most suitable concept for field work is agroforestry using a systems approach and farm planning;
- a committed field team is absolutely essential. The field team maintained consistency and interest in difficult times when it seemed the project could not survive;
- incorporating women in the project, who carried out specific tasks in the family plots, definitely increased the social effectiveness of the project;
- results were improved by enlisting teachers and assigning them specific responsibilities and tasks in environmental education, a factor which is now considered essential. The teachers have passed on their knowledge to children, young people and heads of families; and
- training peasants proved to be an excellent development tool, compared with the more traditional methods of agrarian counselling.

7 Chronology

1950s	Beginning of cotton expansion in the region.
1970s	Height of cotton plantation activity.
1979	The Sandinista revolution brings down the Samoza dictatorship.
1980s	Growing problems of wind and water erosion. Huge dust storms engulf Léon, Chinandega and other localities. Floods destroy roads and railways.
1984	Establishment of the Western Erosion Control Plan (PCEO), setting up tens of kilometres of wind breaks to control wind erosion. National elections won by the Sandinistas.
1986–87	Preparation of Héroes y Mártires de Veracruz management plan.
1988	Conversion of IRENA from autonomous institute to ministerial directorate (DIRENA), giving rise to many redundancies (concentration). Establishment of Pikín Guerrero project.
1989	Establishment of Maribios and OLAFO–Manglares projects.
1990	Elections and change of government in Nicaragua. Re-establishment of IRENA as an autonomous institute with ministerial rank.
1990–93	Continuation of projects and dispersion of Héroes y Mártires project.
1992	Transfer of the Pikín Guerrero project as a whole to IRENA.
1993	MARENA set up to replace IRENA.
1994	'Bridging' phase of the Pikín Guerrero project, practically without funding.
1995	Start of third phase of the Pikín Guerrero project. Land-use planning including the highlands.

Talamanca, Costa Rica

Communal Sustainable Development Projects

DAVID LYNCH (ANAI), BENSON BENEGAS (ANAI) AND FLORANGEL VILLEGAS (ANAI) WITH THE ASSISTANCE OF ALBERTO SALAS (IUCN)

1 Introduction

Talamanca is the largest canton (2,810 km², five per cent of the national territory) of the province of Limón in Costa Rica. It contains seven protected areas under different kinds of management, which together account for 49 per cent of the canton's total area. Biodiversity is very high. There is also great cultural and linguistic diversity, with populations of white peasants and indigenous Bríbris and Cabécares, mainly in the interior, and a population of Afro-Caribbean origin on the coast, along with European, Canadian and American residents.

Talamanca has one of the highest poverty rates in the country. The area is economically depressed due to minimum reinvestment of capital from the main productive activities, which are banana plantations, tourism, agriculture and subsistence fishing. The area has only been linked by bridge to the mainland at Limón since 1978. Few institutions are present,

TALAMANCA, COSTA RICA
Population: approximately 20,000
Land area: 281,000 ha
Ecological zones: tropical rainforest, mountains, coast
Main economic activities: bananas, tourism, subsistence agriculture and fishing

although there has been some improvement since 1994.

The first people to begin development work in Talamanca, in1976, were a group of volunteers who established an experimental farm in the community of Gandoca, with the initial objective of carrying out research in natural resources and providing environmental education. By 1984, the group had established sufficient coordination with local bodies to extend the scope of its efforts. In 1983, the initial group set itself up as an NGO with the name ANAI. At that time, it also called for the issuing of land titles and the establishment of the Forest Wildlife Refuge of Gandoca Manzanillo.

It was during this period that the *Monilia* pest in the cocoa plantations caused economic disaster and sparked the communities' interest in finding alternative production outlets, particularly in agroforestry. ANAI fostered local organizational capacity through a great number of community projects, such as nurseries, reforestation, or the recovery of fruit orchards.

The organization is at present working with some 30 local organizations and many other NGOs. Recent achievements include the establishment of 18 communal banks, improvements in infrastructure, training in various aspects of community development, advice to producer groups,

and encouragement for administrative regionalization.

The situation is now considered to have evolved enough for a sustainable development strategy to be created for the canton, including actions aimed at strengthening local self-management capacity. At present the political situation in Costa Rica is favourable for such an undertaking.

2   Scope and Objectives

ANAI's objectives reflect a gradual adaptation to a changing situation in the field. The initial objectives (1976–1983) focused on environmental research and teaching, but in light of the socio-environmental problems of the canton, sustainable economic alternatives in agroforestry became important (1984–1989). As the local saying goes: "Love with hunger does not last". By 1990, the strategy's purpose became more specific, namely to promote alternatives and opportunities for the sustainable development of the communities.

By 1994, with the addition of successful actions and experiments, the objective had developed into the formulation of a sustainable development strategy, backed by actions aimed at strengthening the communities' own capacity for sustainable production and self-management.

3 Relationship to Development Planning

The actions undertaken are not part of any government plan, nor is the strategy for Talamanca set out in a document. The presence of institutions in the area is very limited. An effort is nevertheless being made in the field in coordination with representatives of the Ministry of Education to introduce environmental education, and to merge the National Forest Wildlife Refuge of Gandoca Manzanillo with the Conservation Area of La Amistad run by MIRENEM.

There is a good chance that the sustainable development activities may be integrated with national policies because of several factors: the political framework established at regional level by the Central American Alliance for Sustainable Development; the process of decentralization in the management of natural resources which has occurred with the creation of Conservation Areas; the President's declaration of sustainable development as a development policy for the present legislature (1994–1998); and the government's own efforts, through the Ministry for Rural Development (MDR) and the Ministry of Planning (MIDEPLAN), to devise a development plan based on community assessments.

4 Main results

Several local and regional organizations have developed, based on the principle of sustainability which originated in the process that began ten years ago. They have now generated economic production alternatives, such as the establishment of 24 communal nurseries.

An area of 1,500 hectares was planted with cocoa, part of which has recently been managed as an organic crop, while an additional 300 hectares were planted with fruit trees and 100 hectares with forest.

ANAI promoted the establishment of the Forest Wildlife Refuge of Gandoca-Manzanillo, while calling for the legalization of land holdings for local inhabitants over a total area of 10,000 hectares, both inside and outside the refuge. This was one of the first projects in Latin America to link land tenure guarantees with prospects for conservation and community development.

In 1990, technical and administrative training for the local population was stepped up, and by now 440 farmers have been able to attend the educational farm. Other actions have been aimed at strengthening community management, such as the management and administration of credit, the ability to plan projects and proposals, and accountancy. There wre 18 community banks set up and the 'organic products' label was obtained for the cocoa and banana crops produced by the communities. Other more recent results have been improvements in infrastructure and progress towards administrative regionalization in Talamanca.

Environmental education is also being provided in indigenous schools, working in combination with representatives of the Ministry of Education and local teachers. Interest is being maintained in forest species, such as the green iguana, as well as in research into natural resources, including marine resources such as reefs, shad, lobster and turtles.

5 Lessons Learned

Many lessons were learned over 14 years in a highly dynamic environment:

- successful projects and actions will gradually lead to a culture of sustainable development, but this process takes time. Short-term objectives can be unrealistic.
- sustainable development is a dynamic process, and work should go on simultaneously in activities focused on development and sustainability;
- there cannot be a valid process at the grassroots level if there is not real participation in decision-making at all levels;
- ANAI's investment in the sustainable development of Talamanca will be a mere drop of water in a desert of non-sustainability, if efforts are not combined in strategic alliances; and
- lack of certainty in funding restricts any long-term undertaking or global vision. Financial flexibility and technical support are needed on the part of the agencies contributing the resources.

7   *Chronology*

1976   A group of volunteers initiates projects directed at environmental research and teaching in the region of Talamanca.

1978   Talamanca is linked to the rest of Costa Rica with the completion of the bridge of La Estrella.

1977–83   The group participates in the establishment of the Forest Wildlife Refuge of Gandoca-Manzanillo. It extends its interest to the whole of the canton of Talamanca, and sets itself up as the ANAI (1983). ANAI works with local communities to offer alternatives in agroforestry to offset the economic disaster generated by the *Monilia* pest in cocoa plantations.

1984–89   An effort is made to obtain guarantees for land holdings as a basis for community development and for the conservation of the refuge. Several projects, including 24 local nurseries and many reforestation schemes, significantly increase the organizational capacity of the communities.

1990–92   Significant changes in the economic and political situation, combined with a shortage of funds for projects, lead to a general review of activities. It is suggested that work be directed at strengthening an indigenous process of self-management for sustainable development.

1994   With the favourable political environment in Costa Rica, the situation is considered ripe to initiate the formulation of a sustainable development strategy for the canton.

Case Studies: Caribbean

Guánica Biosphere Reserve,
Puerto Rico
Samaná Biosphere Reserve,
Dominican Republic
Sierra Maestra, Cuba

Guánica Biosphere Reserve, Puerto Rico

Conservation Strategy

MIGUEL CANALS MORA, DEPARTMENT OF
NATURAL RESOURCES, PUERTO RICO
WITH THE ASSISTANCE OF ARTURO LÓPEZ
ORNAT, IUCN

1 Introduction

The Forest Reserve of Guánica, in south-
west Puerto Rico, was established in 1919.
It contains 4,050 hectares of the best dry
sub-tropical forest on the island as well as
the country's greatest diversity of species
and endemic life. In 1981 it was declared
a biosphere reserve.

The Municipality of Guánica, where the
reserve is situated, was isolated from the
rest of the country in the past. The area
has concentrated on sugar cane harvesting
since the beginning of the 20th century.
The reserve did not have any conservation
problems, although it was not accepted by
the inhabitants. In the mid 1980s Puerto
Rico's tourist boom reached isolated
Guánica, bringing with it land speculation, deterioration of the landscape, and
opportunistic, short-sighted, tourism-
based development.

A plan to construct two roads across the
forest and build several hotel centres and

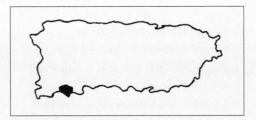

GUÁNICA, PUERTO RICO
Population:
Land area: reserve 4,050 ha; municipality
Ecological zones: dry tropical forest, coast
Main economic activities: sugar cane,
tourism, fishing

secondary residences generated a powerful local movement against the uncontrolled spread of tourism. Supported by local associations, NGOs, the park administration and the local authorities, the movement resorted to whatever means were at hand to publicize the problem and to manifest their opposition; methods such as sit-ins, marches, discussion groups and dialogue with the press were used.

In 1987, they decided to concentrate all their efforts on a local conservation strategy. The strategy was supported by a new Municipal Autonomy Act (1988), which gave municipalities the power to decide on the use and management of land. The aims of the strategy include solving the problem of unwanted tourism, incorporating social development into sustainable production alternatives, organizing tourist routes managed by local organizations, and recovering local history and culture.

As of 1994, the strategy was in the process of participatory formulation. The first actions are being undertaken, such as proposals for the development of pilot projects, the establishment of sectoral working groups and a local advisory committee for the reserve, which is now seen as part of Guánica's common natural and cultural heritage.

2 Objectives and Approach

Initially the objective was the strict protection of what remained of the dry sub-tropical forest. The presence of a common problem, however, in the form of unwanted mass tourism, brought together very different sectors around the issues of conservation and unplanned, non-sustainable development. Since 1987, the working objectives have been extended, the main ones being:

* to make economic development compatible with the conservation of natural resources;
* to preserve the dry sub-tropical forest and foster Guánica's cultural identity;
* to promote the municipality's development by fostering sustainable production practices among the local population;
* to raise environmental awareness in institutions and communities;
* to offer an alternative to mass tourism; and
* to coordinate and organize the different sectors in relation to the strategy, including municipalities, conservation bodies, NGOs and associations.

With the official establishment of municipal autonomy, the strategy may now be classified as local/administrative, with a focus on conservation and development.

3 Relationship to Development Planning

Although the strategy is still in the formulation phase, many of its fundamental principles are well supported in existing Puerto Rican legislation, which combines traditional features with others borrowed from US legislation. The strategy's prospects have been substantially improved by the new Municipal Autonomy Act, which gives municipalities the power to regulate land use. The municipality would act as the authority approving the strategy. The strategy also aims to provide a framework for plans in the sectors of agricultural, forestry, fishing, manufacturing, tourism and education.

4 Initial Development

As outlined earlier, the wave of tourism that Costa Rica experienced began to threaten Guánica in the mid 1980s. By 1987, the central government in consultation with private enterprise was planning to build two roads across the forest, as well as four major hotels, three marinas and several secondary home developments.

The plan generated a powerful local movement against the invasion, formed by local associations, NGOs, the park administration and the municipality. In 1987, they decided to coordinate their efforts in a local conservation strategy, incorporating the recently created Committee for the Rescue of Guánica and other similar groups, cultural centres, the University of Puerto Rico and four political parties (Socialist, New Progressive, Independent and sections of the Partido Popular in power in 1987). The movement was later joined by conservation NGOs, the University of Humacao, the US Forestry Service, Yale University, CANARI, the Municipality of Guánica and a considerable number of private individuals.

The new Municipal Autonomy Act offers a good opportunity to coordinate and manage the strategy. It provides a means of coordinating the work of central government departments which have responsibility for natural resources, with land-use plans prepared at a municipal level. It also opens the door to participation by NGOs, civil associations and community groups, and has led to the establishment of the Guánica Reserve Advisory Committee.

5 Implementation and Results

The strategy identifies and strengthens a number of existing local initiatives, such as diversified agriculture, bee-keeping, small-scale and commercial fishing, ecotourism, and local inhabitants' knowledge and appreciation of the environment. This has helped to develop traditional

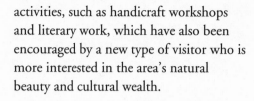

activities, such as handicraft workshops and literary work, which have also been encouraged by a new type of visitor who is more interested in the area's natural beauty and cultural wealth.

The main results achieved to date are:

- agreements and common objectives among different sectors, particularly civil sectors and NGOs, for the area's conservation;
- improved conservation prospects; for instance, a sense of belonging has been developed among the inhabitants with regard to the protected area and a feeling of cultural pride in protecting it as a common heritage of the Municipality of Guánica;
- better information on natural resources in the area;
- a new Biosphere Reserve Advisory Committee; and
- sectoral working groups (fishing, conservation, forestry).

The strategy includes pilot production projects, and also supports other initiatives, such as a museum about the sugar industry, local management of ecological trails, a community marina, etc. Some of the tools used in this process have been:

- an analysis of the many existing legal possibilities;
- public information, protest and presentations in the capital and the press;

- public meetings, technical workshops and work with teachers and schools;
- sectoral working groups and pilot projects in various sectors; and
- support for local initiatives, such as a municipal history museum, and small local tourist organizations.

6 Lessons Learned

Several lessons have been learned from the process:

- participation is stronger if initiated at the start of the process, with shared responsibility for results;
- public participation is essential in a local strategy and must involve all sectors of the community;
- it is vital to work around consensus points, create alliances, make strategic concessions, avoid polarization, and avoid commitment to a single political party or movement;
- use existing organizations, particularly by strengthening them in their sustainable development objectives, and support existing initiatives in the area;
- use the colloquial language of the communities and familiar examples to explain sustainable development and what it means in practical terms; and
- explain the tangible economic, social and cultural benefits to be gained from the conservation of natural resources.

7   Chronology

1919   Creation of the Guánica Forest Reserve of 4,050 hectares to protect a unique dry sub-tropical forest ecosystem, with a high content of biodiversity and endemic life.

1919–80   The Municipality of Guánica is one of the most isolated in Puerto Rico. Its economy revolves around the production of sugar cane and subsistence fishing. The forest reserve is not under pressure.

1980   Puerto Rico promotes and suffers the effects of mass tourism.

1981   The UNESCO MAB declares Guánica a biosphere reserve.

1985   The tourist boom reaches Guánica, attracted by its preserved natural character; government projects for roads and the building of hotels and housing.

1987   Public movement, backed by communities and NGOs in reaction to the impact of tourism, supports greater regulation and respect for local natural and cultural conditions; the movement is later joined by universities, government departments in charge of natural resources and municipal authorities. Decision to initiate a conservation and development strategy for the Municipality of Guánica.

1988   The Municipal Autonomy Act allows municipalities to plan land use and to manage natural resources; the municipality will be the authority approving the strategy.

1991   Sectoral working groups are set up as the embryo of a future Biosphere Reserve Advisory Committee; the strategy formulation process begins alongside the first activities in support of conservation and sustainable development.

Samaná Biosphere Reserve, Dominican Republic

Sustainable Development Strategy

Omar Ramirez Tejada, CEBSE
Rosa A Lamelas, CEBSE
WITH THE ASSISTANCE OF Arturo López, IUCN

1   Introduction

Samaná Bay is the largest bay in the Caribbean. It comprises two protected areas: the Haitises National Park and the Natural Scientific Reserve of Lagunas Redonda y Limón. Every year, from January to March, it is visited by a population of some 1,000 humpback whales (*Megaptera novaeangliae*). This has encouraged the development of a whale-watching industry.

A multi-disciplinary team carried out a mission in 1990; as a result the biosphere reserve of Bahía de Samaná and its surroundings was proposed. The reserve comprised the above-mentioned protected areas, and potentially included a marine core zone for the protection of humpback whales. The biosphere reserve will include Samaná Bay and its land surroundings, covering a total area of 5,204 km², with a population of 246,835 inhabitants (1991

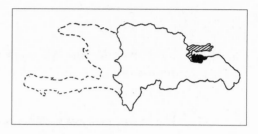

SAMANÁ, DOMINICAN REPUBLIC
Population: 248,000
Land area: 520,400 ha
Ecological zones: tropical coastal flatland, wide bays
Main economic activities: tourism, sugar cane, fishing, agriculture

census). The proposal defines and justifies the core, buffer and transition zones.

In 1991, the Centre for the Conservation and Ecodevelopment of the Bay of Samaná and its Surroundings (CEBSE) was set up as an NGO to catalyze the process. The centre's objectives include establishing the biosphere reserve while involving the communities in project planning and implementation. CEBSE took steps to restructure the Dominican MAB Committee, which was formally established in 1992 by Decree No 136–92.

In 1993, a multi-disciplinary group of professionals came together to undertake an assessment of the area in light of the area's future management. Students and local people were brought into the field work and were kept informed of the results through discussions and pamphlets. An outline management plan was prepared in 1994, and drafts were circulated to the different sectors involved, including representatives of the communities.

Field actions resulting from the assessments proved extremely useful in terms of achieving credibility and gaining the trust of the communities. Particularly effective actions included a campaign to clean up the beaches and municipal control over harassment of whales in the bay. CEBSE focused part of its work on environmental education programmes for young people and teachers and on participatory research conducted on the theme of women and the environment.

Since 1995, the government has been studying the possibility of setting up decentralized planning bodies, initially as pilot projects, in three areas of the country. One of the selected areas is Samaná. The Provincial Planning Council of Samaná, which also comprises representatives from business, production and non-governmental sectors, would be the ideal body to promote the emerging conservation and sustainable development strategy for the area.

2   Objectives and Approach

The focus of the strategy is on land-use planning and establishing a zoning system based on criteria of land capability. It will recommend alternatives to non-sustainable farming activities in surrounding areas, regulate the development of tourism, seek greater local participation and promote the regionalization of development planning.

The main objective of the strategy is to establish a regional cooperation framework to ensure the conservation of biodiversity and improve the quality of life of local communities through appropriate management of natural resources. More specific objectives are to promote economically profitable and environmentally sustainable activities, with greater local participation, as well as the self-financing of programmes for the protection and management of the area.

3   Relationship to Development Planning

In the Dominican Republic, nature conservation has traditionally been a form of protection organized without the participation of local communities. Although buffer zones are not legal entities, a biosphere reserve can be officially recognized. The National Committee for MAB has to evaluate the project and give its approval. The proposal is then submitted to the government for approval by Presidential Decree. The recent political instability has delayed the approval of the strategy; it was submitted to the MAB in 1994, but as of May 1995 had gone no further.

In 1994 the Department of Tourism set up a decentralized Provincial Tourism Commission for the region of Samaná, with the power to recommend sectoral policies and to regulate tourist activities in the area. Representatives of the private tourist sector and NGOs also sit on the commission, and CEBSE supplies the secretariat.

From an institutional point of view the situation improved when the government decided to decentralize three pilot regions. One of them was Samaná; it was chosen because planning had already begun in the area. A Planning Council for the Region of Samaná (COPLASA) was set up, with representatives of all five productive sectors. COPLASA was thought to be the ideal body to promote the emerging conservation and sustainable development strategy for the area.

4   Initial Development

The initial idea arose from a scientific interest in preserving the reserve's biodiversity. Since 1991, CEBSE has been in charge of coordinating the establishment of the biosphere reserve, and has acted as a mediator and a forum for the settlement of conflicts. A proposal document was completed in 1992 by a team of government, NGO and international technical specialists.

A move then began to involve the communities, with the objective of obtaining their views and experience and establishing a common agenda. Tourist activity, especially the whale-watching industry, began to be regulated through consultation with those involved. At the same time, an assessment and strategy for the development of ecotourism was prepared for the region.

An assessment of the fishing sector was also drawn up as part of a project aimed at promoting joint management of fishing in the region. Fishermen were trained and meetings and workshops were held to prepare a work plan for the sector.

5   Implementation and Results

The document prepared by the management committee in 1990 and published in 1992 supported the proposal to set up the biosphere reserve. The proposal was used as a conceptual planning framework for the tourist sector. It also served to activate the restructuring of the MAB Committee, which had been set up in 1976 but had not operated for over a decade.

Although the development phase of the strategy has not yet been completed, some results have been obtained in the course of field work. Since 1994 in particular, CEBSE has encouraged the local population to participate in the areas's planning and management. After CEBSE completed a socio-economic diagnosis of the region, the results were presented to the local communities. These results will subsequently be submitted to the government in order to highlight the importance of participation in the management of the reserve, and to gain official support for this more participatory approach. CEBSE has also set up a database, which it shares with local and central government depart-

ments. The fisheries working group has drawn up a work plan and is currently preparing one for tourism.

Other noteworthy results have been achieved by the environmental education programmes, teacher training and the grant of assistant teacher posts to students staying on as volunteers. In addition, CEBSE completed a participatory gender assessment to determine the role played by Samaná women in the use of natural resources for domestic and economic purposes. In the course of this process, seven community organizers of the Council of Samaná Peasants' Associations (JACASA) were trained in the techniques of participatory research. The aim is to obtain more information about the situation of women and to train them so that they can take part in formulating the regional management plan.

As a result of community participation activities, CEBSE has helped to set up community committees in three of the four main towns of the region. These committees are currently working in support of the biosphere reserve.

6   Lessons Learned

Opportunities include the following:

- international interest for the biosphere reserve; and

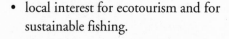

- local interest for ecotourism and for sustainable fishing.

Limitations were as follows:

- no legislative framework for buffer zone designation;
- duplication of tasks and lack of institutional coordination;
- initial distrust on the part of the local population towards conservation and the reserves;
- little social organization or tradition of community participation;
- lack of training programmes;
- over-dependence on a single NGO; and

- shortage of funds and lack of equipment.

Lessons learned during the process include:

- the communities, their representatives and NGOs who have shared responsibility for participating in the management of protected areas have shown an increased interest in the natural values of the area; and
- agreements are convenient instruments to ensure shared responsibility for actions requiring cooperation among institutions.

7   Chronology

1990   A scientific mission proposes the creation of a biosphere reserve.

1991   CEBSE set up; objectives include catalyzing the process.

1992   Dominican MAB Committee restructured; CEBSE publishes a summary of the proposal to establish the biosphere reserve.

1993   Basic field data obtained to support a proposal for the management of the area. Idea of a biosphere reserve publicized in the region.

1994   Initiation of environmental education and community participation programme; participatory research with groups of women. Biosphere reserve proposal submitted to national MAB Committee for evaluation and, if appropriate, forwarding to the government. Department of Tourism sets up a decentralized Provincial Tourism Commission for the Region of Samaná, with the participation of the business sector and NGOs. Commission secretariat provided by CEBSE. Campaign to clean up beaches and control whale-watching activities (initiated in 1992) intensifies.

1995   The government considers setting up a decentralized body, on a pilot basis, in the Samaná Region. The body, called COPLASA, will have participation from government, business and NGOs. A possibility arises of setting up a protected marine area on the north coast of the Samaná peninsula with the participation of the tourist sector.

Sierra Maestra, Cuba

Conservation and Development Strategy, National System of Protected Areas

ANTONIO PERERA PUGA, COMARNA (CUBA)
PEDRO ROSABAL GONZALEZ, COMARNA
(CUBA) WITH THE ASSISTANCE OF ARTURO LÓPEZ
ORNAT, IUCN

SIERRA MAESTRA, CUBA
Population: 60,000 families
Land area: 530,000 ha
Ecological zones: seasonal, tropical
mountains 200-2,000 m
Main economic activities: coffee, cocoa,
cattle, timber, mining, tourism

1 Introduction

Cuba is the largest island in the West Indies and has the greatest biodiversity in the Caribbean. The Sierra Maestra is Cuba's largest mountain range, encompassing part of the provinces of Granma, Santiago de Cuba and Guantánamo. It is 250 km long and 30 km wide at its broadest part; it covers a total area of 530,000 hectares, with altitudes of between 200 and 2000 m above sea level. Because of its relief, geomorphology, hydrological structure, soils, climate and vegetation, it forms a complex and fragile ecological system.

The National System of Protected Areas (SINAP) was set up in 1990 to complete the representation of protected areas, contribute to national socio-economic development and environmental awareness, and strengthen institutional capacity for these objectives. The creation of

SINAP resulted from the success of the sustainable development and conservation strategy for the Sierra Maestra, which began in 1980.

Until 1980, the area was exposed to colonization and forested areas were converted into pasture and plots of land for migratory agriculture. This resulted in negative repercussions for soil erosion and regulation of the water supply.

The conservation strategy was started under Law No 27 (1980), with the aim of regulating soil erosion, ensuring the preservation of biodiversity, and improving the standard of living and socio-economic conditions of the area's inhabitants. The strategy was formulated in 1984 and revised in 1991. It provides guidelines for the area's development and is fully integrated with the national development planning system.

A territorial plan was drawn up on the basis of nine categories of land-use capacity, establishing 14 core zones totalling 250,000 hectares. Buffer zones are being developed by a combination of local government, communities and citizens' committees of different kinds through programmes of environmental education, infrastructure improvements, reforestation (approximately 4000 hectares annually since 1984), and general support for the agricultural and tourist sectors. This strategy served as a test case and

general framework for other protected areas in Cuba, and contributed to the setting up of the National System of Protected Areas.

The process has been based entirely on national technical and financial resources. The Cuban government (acting through six ministries), the National Environmental Commission (COMARNA), the Physical Planning Institute (IPF), provincial governments, the 13 relevant municipalities and the National Small Farmers Association (ANAP) were mainly responsible for formulating the strategy and for preparing and implementing annual action plans in consultation with the communities.

The process has led to effective intersectoral collaboration, undoubtedly facilitated by Cuba's centralised planning system. The main limitation has been the difficult economic situation generated by the international embargo, which hampers the allocation of budgets and reduces the availability of staff for technical training work.

2 Objectives and Approach

This is a governmental strategy, local in scope, aimed at the conservation and sustainable development of the main mountainous region of Cuba. Because of the area's geographical characteristics, it

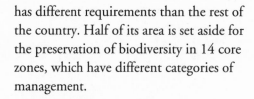

has different requirements than the rest of the country. Half of its area is set aside for the preservation of biodiversity in 14 core zones, which have different categories of management.

The main objective of the strategy is 'to protect historical/cultural and natural values and foster comprehensive, harmonious development' within the boundaries of the area officially known as the Great National Park of Sierra Maestra.

Specific objectives are:

- conservation and study of biodiversity in the Sierra Maestra;
- regulation of land use;
- protection of soils and water catchment areas;
- protection of the countryside and reforestation;
- socio-economic development of inhabitants;
- environmental education and awareness;
- recreation and tourism; and
- enhancing places of historical/cultural interest.

The strategy formulated in 1984 established new inter-sectoral coordination mechanisms at the national level, as well as coordination between national bodies and provincial, municipal, communal and citizens' organizations.

3 Relationship to Development Planning

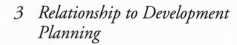

Because of its structure, the Sierra Maestra strategy relies on official institutions already connected with regional activities. Under the 1980 law, ANAP – the main NGO in the area – also plays a part in planning and decision-making.

The strategy provides guidelines for the region's development and is fully integrated with the national development planning system. The Cuban government, acting through its agencies, is responsible for preparing and implementing yearly action plans.

The system of protected areas was set up in 1990 by COMARNA. COMARNA is composed of the 22 governmental organizations and five NGOs most closely connected with this sector, and was made official by decree that same year. The related regulations await approval by the State Council and National Assembly. The management of SINAP is coordinated by COMARNA, in conjunction with two ministries, three national institutes and local authorities. Work is carried out through provincial environmental commissions, and inter-sectoral working groups have been set up to coordinate and strengthen the combined efforts of participants. Each member body of COMARNA is in charge of imple-

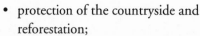
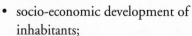
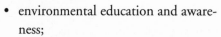

menting and monitoring those strategy tasks which fall within its area of responsibility. COMARNA supervises the strategy as a whole. Any disagreement which cannot be resolved within the commission is referred to the Council of Ministers.

4   Initial Development

From the 18th century on, the Sierra Maestra was colonized and significantly affected by inappropriate use of land, particularly in the form of migratory agriculture and most recently by the expansion of cattle farming. Such activity affected almost 40 per cent of the mountainous region. This has caused serious erosion, sedimentation and loss of water regulation capability. Various water catchment areas, including Cauto, the largest in Cuba, originate in this mountain, with associated systems of drinking-water storage and supply, hydroelectric production, agricultural irrigation and fish farming, which is of great importance to the eastern part of the island.

Not only was the ecological equilibrium of the mountain areas affected, but a socio-economic imbalance arose due to emigration to the flatlands. These emigrants abandoned coffee and cocoa cultivation and caused an excessive demand for employment and services in the cities.

In 1980 a law was passed declaring the region a 'protected rural area' (IUCN category VIII) to be called Gran Parque Nacional Sierra Maestra, with the objectives of sustainable development and conservation. Since then, two prospective development proposals for the park have been issued, one in 1984 and another in 1991.

The first of these proposals (1984) is based on an analysis of the region's problems and sets forth regulations for land use, conservation, forestry and farming development. It is also a strategy for socio-economic development, covering aspects such as population, production and employment, human settlement, social services and infrastructure. Its guidelines were used in planning and operations until 1991, when approval was given at inter-ministerial level to the proposal for prospective development to the year 2000. This was an update of the previous proposal, including some new sectors such as tourism.

The action plans cover three basic fields:

- environment and natural and historical/cultural resources;
- economy and infrastructure; and
- population and services.

Part of the methodology projected eight- to ten-year scenarios (1984–1991 and

1991–2000), with a view to analyzing situations and scenarios specific to the region and neighbouring provinces. These were developed in light of the need to readjust plans for human settlements, review the supply of labour and economic fundamentals, furnish adequate economic incentives and propose new regulations. Local political divisions and ecological units and catchment areas provided the framework for action proposals. Once action priorities had been identified, investments were earmarked accordingly and operational resources, incentives and grants were allocated to local authorities, communities and producer groups. Plans were implemented by national technical staff and financed entirely by national resources.

An inter-disciplinary governmental group prepared the draft legislation and set up a steering committee, which was dependent on the Council of Ministers and assisted by a technical advisory board. The board's specialists are responsible for analyzing tasks and plans and for monitoring implementation. Both the steering committee and the technical advisory board include representatives and specialists of the 20 organisations involved in the development of the region.

The steering committee's component bodies are responsible for financing and implementing projects. They are the Ministries of Agriculture, Basic Industry,

Transport, Construction, Public Health and Communications. The National Institute of Tourism, the Physical Planning Institute and the People's Provincial and Municipal Organs (from three provinces and 13 municipalities) are also represented.

Work is carried out through these organizations and, as is often the case in Cuba, is supported by civic associations such as the Defense, Federation and Cuban Women's Committees, schools, and ANAP. On the basis of a priority action schedule, the technical team adapts annual plans to different scenarios according to the availability of funds.

A number of sociological indicators are monitored each year as a means of identifying changes in local conditions. The technical team decided to use the same indicators as those used by the Ministry of Agriculture and the Central Planning Council, in order to establish a common language and ensure reliability of data. Results tend to indicate that while some conditions improve and some difficulties are resolved, other problems appear.

Bringing the strategy to the field was not easy. The working methodology was revised three times in order to adapt it to local conditions. The initial 'top-down' concept was gradually combined with a more participatory approach, which allowed feedback in both directions.

Field projects are essentially implemented through the local communities by the above-mentioned committees. The communities are also consulted when it comes to preparing annual action plans. In several cases producer associations contracted the services of forestry experts and agronomists.

The nature of the Cuban system of internal organization is particularly favourable to the implementation of a sustainable development strategy, particularly from the point of view of long-term planning, inter-sectoral coordination, the application of investment and incentive regulations and policies, and the participation of rural and urban populations. These conditions cannot really be extrapolated to other countries in the region.

The founding of SINAP was due in large part to the success of the Sierra Maestra experiment, as well as the Ciénaga de Zapata (the archipelago's most extensive wetland) and other land and marine areas. A further vital contribution was a national assessment of protected areas (Perera, A. and P. Rosabal. (1987). *Estudio integral de la Sierra Maestra.* Comisión Nacional del Medio Ambiente y los Recursos Naturales (COMARNA). Havana, Cuba), along with the hosting of a national workshop in 1989, which produced the recommendation of the technical group responsible for proposing the system.

5   Implementation and Results

Two of the most visible results of the Sierra Maestra strategy are the introduction of an environmental awareness to socio-economic development planning and the establishment of a structure ensuring inter-sectoral coordination. The strategy has served as a test and general framework for other protected areas in Cuba, particularly the Ciénaga de Zapata, and has given national status to the system of protected areas. The Sierra Maestra strategy was the first planning methodology developed for mountainous regions in Cuba and marked the first time that an inter-disciplinary study of this particular area was undertaken. This eventually led to the Prospective Development Proposal (PDP) for 1984–1991.

The 1984–1991 PDP proposed nine categories of use, identifying some areas for strict conservation (36 per cent of the region), some for limited forestry and tourist use (14 per cent) and some for diversified use (the remainder). The conservation areas cover nearly 250,000 hectares and are composed of different categories of protected area: six nature reserves, four national parks, three wildlife refuges and eleven areas for tourist use. Currently only four of these areas (three parks and a refuge) have a management plan and/or assigned personnel.

In the areas allocated to diversified use, there are 60,000 dwellings (equivalent to some four hectares per family) distributed over nearly 1,000 settlements. Electrification in these settlements has increased from 21 to 70 per cent. One-third of the area is intended for agricultural use, (mainly cocoa and coffee), the rest for fruit growing and subsistence agriculture. Initially the project's technical team concentrated on achieving agricultural results in a series of pilot farms. Most of the remaining 170,000 hectares are still used for cattle, although it is planned to reduce this area to 90,000 hectares. This would be more in line with land-use capacity and would take account of genetic advances resulting in increased milk production.

Tens of thousands of hectares in the area were restored for use by replacing secondary vegetation with forest and/or coffee and cocoa plantations. Since 1980, more than 30,000 hectares have been reforested in this way and the proportion of forested land is due to be increased to 50 per cent of the total area by the year 2000. The most common species are *Pinus maestrensis, Pinus caribaea*, deciduous trees such as *Hibiscus elatus* and, to a lesser extent, eucalyptus. Some areas are devoted to mining; their ecological recovery is planned once exploitation has been completed. The promotion of tourism has been extended to 1482 lodgings in 13 communities, a number which is expected to rise significantly in the future.

SINAP has also achieved significant results; it now covers some 12 per cent of the national territory. SINAP has been integrated into national development policies through the National Environment and Development Programme, which was presented by Cuba at UNCED, and forms part of Cuba's commitments to Agenda 21 and the Biodiversity Convention.

SINAP's development has been based entirely on national technical and financial capabilities. Each sector contributes part of the resources required for its maintenance. Currently, the most heavily-visited protected areas help to finance the maintenance of those with more restricted use. Since 1989, the economic problems generated by the international embargo have made it difficult to allocate the necessary funds and to assign staff to technical training work. These problems have also seriously weakened the areas' management programmes and in some remote areas have brought about a return to non-sustainable subsistence production.

6 Lessons Learned

Main factors against the strategy include:

- the lack of regulations, which have been prepared but still await approval by the Council of Ministers;

- the implementation of large-scale public works was not always in keeping with environmental conditions;
- the economic problems generated by the embargo, particularly since 1989, prevented the allocation of planned funds, created circumstances conducive to non-sustainable subsistence production, and caused a scarcity of technical personnel to disseminate the results of research into stable production alternatives such as fish farming and agroforestry; and
- for SINAP, initial limiting factors included the sectoral conservation approach adopted by both specialists and institutions, and the unfamilarity of the concept of sustainable development applied to protected areas.

The main opportunities for the development of the process have been:

- the richness and fragility of the area's ecosystems, combined with gradual depopulation and the area's marginal economic situation before 1980, which drew attention to its development prospects;
- centralised planning, which ensured strong collaboration between government institutions in all sectors;
- the existence of a high-level environmental commission and an extensive committee structure at community and citizen level; and

- Cuba's commitment to Agenda 21 and the Biodiversity Convention, especially for SINAP.

The principal lessons learned were:

- the importance of a methodology in which categories of land use are assigned in accordance with the characteristics and capacities of the region;
- the need for inter-sectoral analysis of conservation and development problems;
- the need for broad consultation with the affected populations for their assessment of the socio-environmental situation and their outlook;
- the desirability, during the diagnosis stage, of determining priorities for the implementation of programmes in consultation with communities, and of applying corrective action rapidly to overcome specific problems;
- the use of research/action based on model plots of land, as a basis for technical training and dissemination, which should be given priority over or at least be equal to basic biological research; and
- the importance of a comprehensive appraisal in the analysis of the system as a whole, rather than on a case-by-case basis, and the need for action plans to be kept flexible and adaptable to the conditions of time and place.

7   *Chronology*

pre 1980   Spontaneous colonization of the Sierra Maestra, deforestation, extensive livestock rearing and subsistence agriculture in mountainous regions poorly suited to such activity.

1980   Act passed creating the Sierra Maestra Protected Rural Area, covering 500,000 hectares, aimed at conservation and sustainable development. Creation of an inter-ministerial steering committee and a technical advisory board, composed of more than 20 national and local organizations, including six ministries.

1980-84   Implementation of the first prospective development proposal 1984–1991 by technical teams in consultation with the Sierra Maestra population.

1984   Application of the strategy, establishing a territorial plan based on nine categories of use; 14 protected areas and one multiple-use area instituted on 250,000 hectares for the purpose of sustainable development, with inter-sectoral cooperation mechanisms.

1987   National assessment of protected areas.

1984-90   Management plans for four of the Sierra Maestra protected areas. Development of applied research into productive aspects of agroforestry; reforestation of 8,000 hectares yearly, recovery of abandoned wells and relocation of crops; fostering of evergreen wooded areas; development of 1,432 lodgings for tourists in 13 Sierra communities.

1989   National workshop for protected areas; technical group placed in charge of the SINAP proposal.

1990   Creation of the National System for the Protection of the Environment; constitution of the national technical group for protected areas and approval of SINAP by COMARNA.

1991   Second prospective development plan for the Sierra Maestra, 1991–2000.

1992   SINAP is officially included as part of the Cuban contribution to UNCED and its commitment to Agenda 21 and the Convention on Biological Diversity .

1989-93   Severe deterioration in Cuba's economic situation due to the political change in the Soviet bloc, causing a tightening of the blockade to which the country is subjected. Strong budgetary limitations, shortage of technicians, fuel and operational resources. Regression of some communities to subsistence activities and non-sustainable farming.

1993   Inter-institutional and inter-disciplinary working groups at local level. Revision of SINAP to include marine areas.

Case Studies:
South America

Amazonia Project, Ecuador
Sierra Nevada, Colombia
Tambopata-Candamo, Peru
Mata Atlántica/APTA, Brasil

Amazonia Project, Ecuador

Sustainable Development Strategy

Jorge Albán Gomez, Natura Foundation
Augusto Angel Maya, IUCN–SUR
With the assistance of Arturo López,
IUCN

1 Introduction

Over the last three decades Ecuadorian Amazonia has been dramatically affected by several developments, including the impact of the petroleum industry (which produces 50 per cent of Ecuador's GDP in this area alone) as well as colonization, timber extraction and cattle-raising. The area covers 140,000 km² and has 450,000 inhabitants. Annual deforestation amounts to 70,000 hectares, and over one million hectares have already been converted to pasture. Approximately 40 per cent of the area is designated protected land; for example indigenous reserves, forest reserves, or forest areas. Legal indigenous reserves account for four million hectares.

As an exporter of raw materials, the area presents a typical profile of an economy deprived of reinvestment. The national government does not have any specific

AMAZONIA, ECUADOR
Population: 450,000
Land area: 14,000,000 ha
Ecological zones: Amazonian rainforest, rivers
Main economic activities: petrol, timber, cattle, subsistence agriculture

policies for developing the region, local organizations are politically weak, and all middle-range decisions are taken by the central government. It could be argued that only the indigenous peoples in the region have a strong sense of purpose and tradition.

The process of formulating a sustainable development strategy for Amazonia began in 1993 as a result of IUCN initiatives, wide-ranging consultations, and the involvement of the Natura Foundation. The strategy is currently in the stage of formulation and negotiation with local and national players.

The joint IUCN–Natura Foundation team organized five regional forums, one for each of Ecuadorian Amazonia's administrative provinces. These forums brought together all the players in the area, including local authorities, business and social sectors, indigenous groups, the Church and the military. Indigenous groups were reluctant to cooperate with the government and with some NGOs; the governments of the departments were the most enthusiastic participants.

Sectoral meetings were also organized to prepare practical proposals. The objective of these forums was to prepare a plan of action for each province, with a view to negotiating the plans with the central government. The eventual objective is for the government to formulate a proposal for Amazonia, which can then serve as a basis for negotiations with the timber and oil industries.

The central government recently set up the Institute for the Ecodevelopment of Amazonia (ECORAE), with which IUCN–Natura Foundation made an agreement. Another agreement was signed with the presidential environment committee. However, the aim is for the Amazonian players themselves to defend their proposal. In this phase, the IUCN–Natura Foundation wish to give priority to land-use planning; specific projects (eg experimental farms in Puyo, a joint experiment in Napo, environmental sanitation in several municipalities); communication and environmental education; and strengthening existing projects and bodies, such as the agrarian councils.

Decentralization has been very slow, and although some provinces and municipalities have responded satisfactorily, the process is not yet complete. Other noteworthy limitations so far have been the peasant representatives' perceived lack of legitimacy, and the uneven and feeble nature of the indigenous participation. As of 1995 the situation was further aggravated by a border conflict with Peru.

2 Objectives and Approach

The ultimate objective is the sustainable development of the Amazonian region of Ecuador. Specific objectives are:

- to encourage the participation of all the different players in the process in formulating sustainable development policies for Amazonia;
- to encourage decentralization in decision-making related to the development of Amazonia, seeking to ensure that each province prepares its own development proposals;
- to generate agreements and commitments based on those proposals;
- to promote land-use planning;
- to strengthen existing projects; and
- to promote sustainable development activities.

Methods include:

- organizing provincial forums in the five provinces which involve all players, and submitting proposals to the central government;
- having the government develop an Amazonian proposal through ECORAE based on the proposals from the forums;
- promoting sectoral forums;
- developing specific projects in the areas of production and environmental sanitation; and
- generating and disseminating information concerning the region, particularly through communication and environmental education.

3 Relationship to Development Planning

The strategy is still in the development phase. A plan of action was prepared for each province at provincial forums; these plans will be negotiated with the central government. The aim is for the government to develop a proposal for Amazonia which can serve as a basis for negotiations with the timber and oil industries. Strategy formulation is part of the process of developing a master plan for Amazonia under the responsibility of ECORAE. It is hoped, however, that the Amazonian players themselves will defend their proposals.

4 Initial Development

The process of developing a sustainable development strategy for Amazonia began in 1993. The central strategy group was made up of four professionals, with one promoter in each of the five provinces. The group of professionals included an anthropologist, an economist, an agronomist and a historian. The promoters for three of the provinces (Sucumbíos, Napo

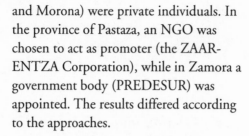

and Morona) were private individuals. In the province of Pastaza, an NGO was chosen to act as promoter (the ZAAR-ENTZA Corporation), while in Zamora a government body (PREDESUR) was appointed. The results differed according to the approaches.

The joint IUCN–Natura Foundation team organized five regional forums. Before each forum was convened, organizations were informed about the project's objectives and their comments were solicited. The results of this effort were uneven.

At each of the provincial forums, participants were asked to circulate their conclusions and thus broaden the scope of the discussion. That did not happen, however, except in a very few cases. This is perhaps an indication that community participation in planning tasks in Amazonia has still not become routine practice. The success of regional forums was heavily dependent on the leadership of some members of the community, and on the organizational capacity and experience of the promoters of the project.

5   Implementation and Results

The strategy has entered the development stage. It was initiated only two years ago, and it is already facing a complex situation, limited by strong externalities. The main result so far has been to promote discussion of, and consensus on, regional development. A process of participatory analysis has been initiated through the provincial forums and the first proposals for submission to the central government are beginning to emerge.

Although some provinces and municipalities have responded well, this type of participatory approach is not yet firmly established. In addition, there is not enough political authority to impose forms of conduct on the different sectors. Decentralization is making very slow progress, although it is still one of the main concerns of the strategy.

The urgent need to arrive at some preliminary agreements has already been stressed, since logging in the area is increasing, with plans to market eight million cubic metres of timber per year. It is feared that it will be no easy task to reconcile the indigenous proposals with those of the provincial governments.

A few specific projects have been started, including studies in social communication, the economic implications of environmental externalities, guidelines for the management of natural forests, an assessment of the legal structure of Amazonian development and possible related structural reforms, an assessment of existing financial instruments and a proposal for gender-related work.

6 Lessons Learned

Limitations included the following:

- an isolated economy (50 per cent of Ecuador's GNP comes from oil). There are plans to extract eight million cubic metres of timber per year;
- political weakness of the highly-centralized national government, and regional governments without proposals of their own;
- very limited means of communication and transportation within the region – it is easier to travel from outside the region than within it;
- an agricultural frontier situation, including lack of land-use planning, colonization without any understanding of the culture of forests, organizational weakness, and powerful technical and financial constraints;
- lack of fair, organized representation for peasants; and
- indigenous people are reluctant to take part in programmes jointly with the government or even with NGOs.

Lessons taught by the process include:

- provincial and municipal governments have been keen to cooperate from the beginning, but the representatives of central government bodies initially lacked enthusiasm;
- indigenous communities were generally reluctant and distrustful at the first meetings. The players were not involved in participatory planning proposals. This was due to a great extent to the centralized nature and paternalism of the state;
- the best response came from sectors with a focused planning framework, political consistency and personal leadership. For instance, the response of local governments was more effective than that of provincial councils;
- the representatives of social groups seldom passed on information from the discussions to their organizations;
- the success of provincial planning forums depended to a great extent on the participation of a representative of the Ministry for Agriculture and Stockbreeding (MAG); and
- it is best not to go to meetings with any pre-established notion of what regional development should be.

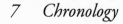

7   *Chronology*

1970   Beginnings of colonization, driven by oil exploration activities.

1987   Agrarian councils set up in Ecuador, involving all official national and regional bodies dealing with the farming sector, and attended by social organizations without the right to vote.

1993   IUCN and the Natura Foundation initiate the process for the formulation of a strategy.

1994   Plans for the annual extraction of eight million cubic metres of timber. Provincial forums held in the five Amazonian provinces. Support for the 'Broad Front for the Defence of Amazonia', whose main aim is to control the activities of the oil industry and their impact on indigenous lands.

1995   Publication of first newsletters: 'The Future of Amazonia'. Strengthening of agrarian councils and some specific projects: experimental farm in Puyo, shared experience in Napo, environmental sanitation at Lago Agrio, Tena and Puyo, communication by means of newsletters in two provinces, and environmental education committees in three provinces. Armed border conflict with Peru.

Sierra Nevada de Santa Marta, Colombia

Conservation Strategy for Tropical Forests

Juan Mayr, Guillermo Rodriguez, Natalia Ortiz, Hernando Sanchez, Pro-Sierra Foundation, with the assistance of Robert Prescott-Allen, IUCN–CESP

1 Introduction

The Sierra Nevada de Santa Marta rises sharply from the Caribbean coast; in just 42 km its snowy peaks reach a height of 5,775 m. It covers an area of 17,000 km² and is the highest coastal mountain range in the world, separated from the main Andes range by flat, semi-arid regions.

Due to its size, variation in altitude, location and isolated nature, the Sierra Nevada is important from a hydrological and biological point of view. It is the 'water factory' for 35 water catchment areas, which supply about one and a half million inhabitants in the plains. Its tropical rainforests, dry tropical forests and many other habitats are representative of most of the ecosystems of tropical America. There is a rich diversity of species; 20 to 40 per cent of them are endemic. Part of the Sierra Nevada is a national park and biosphere reserve. The

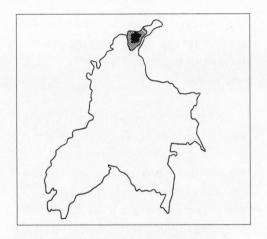

SIERRA NEVADA, COLOMBIA
Population: 190,000
Land area: 1,700,000 ha
Ecological zones: seasonal tropics, from sea level to 5,775 m
Main economic activities: coffee, subsistence agriculture, cattle, marijuana; bananas and cotton in surrounding flatlands

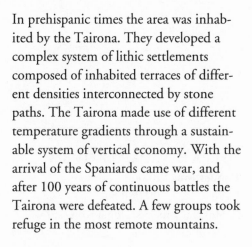
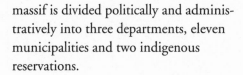

massif is divided politically and administratively into three departments, eleven municipalities and two indigenous reservations.

In prehispanic times the area was inhabited by the Tairona. They developed a complex system of lithic settlements composed of inhabited terraces of different densities interconnected by stone paths. The Tairona made use of different temperature gradients through a sustainable system of vertical economy. With the arrival of the Spaniards came war, and after 100 years of continuous battles the Tairona were defeated. A few groups took refuge in the most remote mountains.

Because of the difficulty experienced by Europeans who tried to settle in the mountains of the interior, the remaining indigenous groups managed to live in relative isolation until the end of the 19th century. Three indigenous groups, the Ijka, Kogui and Sanja, live in the high mountainous area, with a total population of 30,000 inhabitants. The Kogui and some of the Ijka retain their pre-Colombian traditions, while the others are being rapidly deprived of their culture. Another 160,000 people from various regions live in the middle and lower ranges of the mountains. Many settled there over the last 50 years to escape the crisis unleashed in the 1940s by the fall in the price of bananas, which was the main lowland

crop, and to avoid the sectarian violence in the interior of the country at that time.

During the 1970s, thousands of hectares of forest were cleared to grow marijuana, which offered an economic return at least ten times greater than that of coffee. The government countered by partially eradicating the crops with herbicides. This was also an era marked by a resurgence of violence. Some settlers left the land; others returned to growing coffee, still others started growing coca. In the 1980s land was abandoned, conflicts were polarized and exacerbated, the soil was impoverished and erosion continued. National government was either absent or repressive. Guerrillas emerged to fill the vacuum left by the government, competing for territorial control with paramilitary groups which had appeared during the marijuana boom.

Nowadays, indigenous people, peasants, settlers, businessmen, guerrillas and other dwellers of the Sierra Nevada form a mixed society with different values and interests. There is little if any cooperation among them.

The principal causes of the impoverishment of the Sierra Nevada resource base are the rapid destruction of the forests, the introduction of unsuitable production systems, inappropriate technology, continued drug cultivation, the lack of a national government presence and poor coordination between the three departmental governments and 11 municipalities of the region. Only 15 per cent of the primary forest remains. The loss of the forests has had disastrous consequences for the region's hydrology, affecting both the supply of water to neighbourhood communities and the irrigation of large farming areas.

The Pro-Sierra Nevada de Santa Marta Foundation was founded in 1986 with the aim of halting environmental damage and promoting conservation of the Sierra. The foundation is a non-profit NGO. The central government and the departmental and municipal authorities share the foundation's organization and work with business representatives, indigenous communities, peasants, scientists and private individuals.

Since 1987, the foundation has carried out a restoration programme for the Sierra Nevada de Santa Marta. In the first stage it completed a comprehensive diagnosis on the basis of available information and generated new information about the region, covering its history since the 15th century and its institutional, ecological, political, economic, cultural and territorial aspects.

The foundation has set up two ecological stations, one inside the park, the other on the border. Their principal objectives are to provide protection for the park, undertake ecological research, study ethnic relations and forest regeneration, and promote appropriate technologies in collaboration with local populations.

The foundation has also established two community care centres. The Congo Centre works with a peasant community on preventative health, mother and infant care, sanitation, training, organization, agro-ecology, fish farming and archaeological research and restoration. More than 100 reservoirs have been set up for fish breeding in an effort to reduce the high level of infant malnutrition. The Shimelumke Centre is located in one of the most impoverished areas of the Sierra, with a population of indigenous peoples, peasants and mixed races. Violence in the area has grown in response to the enlargement of the indigenous reservation and has limited the scope of the centre to monitoring the situation. In 1993, the centre had to suspend activities on account of public unrest.

In 1991 the foundation recognized the need for a broader and more participatory strategy. Its action focused on disseminating information and providing training for the different players – indigenous people, peasants, businessmen, politicians, governmental and NGOs – in order to strengthen their ability to take action, with the ultimate aim of halting the deterioration of the Sierra Nevada. The

foundation's management is now working to institutionalize the strategy; there is (1995) a preliminary draft document already in place.

2 Scope and Objectives

The objective of the strategy is to strengthen the coordination and action capacity of the communities and of governmental and non-governmental organizations in order to halt the deterioration of, and improve ecological and socio-economic conditions in, the Sierra Nevada. This is the start of a participatory process to lay the foundations of a conservation strategy and sustainable development plan for the area.

Specific objectives are:

- to better inform the players concerned and the public about the Sierra Nevada's environmental, institutional, legislative, and socio-economic processes;
- to establish mechanisms for cooperation and coordination between institutions for the management of the Sierra Nevada's natural resources;
- to improve the standard of living of the inhabitants and guarantee security of land tenure for indigenous communities and the security of their holy sites;
- to plan land uses and resolve conflicts between interest groups;

- to seek to establish a single administrative body for the Sierra Nevada;
- to promote the use of appropriate technology;
- to preserve biodiversity and the water regulation capacity of ecosystems, particularly their role in water supply, through cooperative action; and
- to set in motion a sustainability monitoring and evaluation process.

3 Relationship to Development Planning

In 1995, following consultation with the different parties, the National Planning Department initiated the formulation of a draft document. Efforts have continued to develop a mechanism for institutionalizing the strategy's recommendations and results, thus providing the basis for a sustainable development plan for the Sierra Nevada. Work is progressing on three levels.

1. At the national level, through the National Planning Department and the Ministry of the Environment, by setting up Corposierra (by law) and negotiating its recognition as the coordinator of the sustainable development plan, in accordance with the results and guidelines produced by the strategy.
2. At a departmental level, through the Regional Planning Council for the

Atlantic Coast (CORPES) and the National Rehabilitation Plan (PNR), renamed the Social Solidarity Network in accordance with the new government plan, in a project to include the massif as an environmental priority area in central government policy and to promote the introduction of an environmental component in departmental and municipal development plans.

3. At the municipal level, a project was undertaken under the PNR to set up the Association of Sierra Nevada Municipalities (Asosierra), with the aim of joint environmental action in the massif. Asosierra is now operational and a second phase of consolidation is underway.

In addition, an inventory is being drawn up of the programmes and projects of other governmental and non-governmental organizations, with a view to analyzing them and establishing coordinated action. Meanwhile, an effort is being made with NGOs to set up an association to ensure the feedback of experience and joint planning in the Sierra Nevada.

4   Initial Development

Initial work on the strategy began in 1992, with a series of consultation meetings throughout the region supported by the Swedish Nature Society. In 1993, with the financial support of GTZ and technical assistance from IUCN, the foundation began to formulate a conservation strategy for the tropical forests of the Sierra Nevada de Santa Marta. The strategy aimed to lay the foundations for a sustainable development plan for the region, with international sources providing 90 per cent of funding. An all-Colombian team of 34 people has been set up to prepare the strategy.

Participating organizations include the Colombian government (represented by the National Planning Department), CORPES-Atlantic Coast, the Ministry of the Environment and other local organizations working in the area, such as the recently created Asosierra, the Association of Peasant Leaders of the Sierra Nevada (Asolideres) and the indigenous organization Gonawindua Tayrona.

5   Implementation and Results

Although the strategy is not in a phase of formal implementation, it has generated guidelines which are starting to be assimilated by official institutions in their policies, plans and programmes (section 3). The strategy is chiefly a process for reaching consensus. Participation and environmental education are two of the main tools used in recreational and discussion workshops with communities. Other tools frequently used include the mass media, such as radio and newspapers, informative literature, videos, audio-visual presentations, theatre performances, puppets and musical festivals. By giving priority to working with indigenous and peasant communities, institutions and unions; by consulting them and providing information; by creating awareness and offering training, the process has generated a series of mechanisms to ensure continued participation.

This type of joint approach is intended to add real viability to the regional plan, which will be proposed after consultation with the players. The approach will also facilitate the conclusion of practical agreements on the use of natural resources.

A first draft of the general conservation strategy document is ready. This document, which covers the process and the various points of view and approaches of those involved, will then be resubmitted to the groups for their opinions. After that, a final version should emerge, which will further facilitate agreement and which will be incorporated into a sustainable regional development plan.

6 Lessons Learned

A strategy dealing with dynamic groups and interests should itself be dynamic. Dynamism is not generally associated with the preparation of documents, and a

documentary strategy might therefore appear to be a waste of time. Between 1987 and 1991, the Pro-Sierra Nevada de Santa Marta Foundation operated with some degree of success using an implicit strategy. Since 1993, however, it has been considered preferable to implement an explicit strategy, since only an explicit version can be shared, developed and implemented with a broad range of participants.

People need incentives to participate in a strategy. One means of providing this is to focus on an issue that every (or nearly every) potential participant agrees with: in this case, the value of water and the role of forests in safeguarding the quality and supply of water.

Having worked with all the key players, raising awareness, informing and training were found to be insufficient. There was also a need to strengthen their internal management and negotiating abilities, even at municipal and institutional levels. That is to say, it was necessary to first work within each organization (internal consultation) before seeking to reach a consensus among them, so that when the time came to implement the strategy, the necessary mechanisms would already be in place. The strategy requires political will at all levels, and the failure to obtain this support at a national, regional or local level may bring the process to a standstill.

7   Chronology

1986   Creation of the Pro-Sierra Nevada de Santa Marta Foundation.

1987   The foundation sets up the first ecological station; its aims include protecting areas of great diversity and ecological importance and involving the communities.

1988   The foundation carries out a comprehensive assessment of the Sierra Nevada.

1989   The foundation sets up the community care centre, promoting a comprehensive methodology of research and action with local communities.

1991   The foundation recognizes the need for a broader and more participatory strategy that incorporates other sectors, including government.

1992   Work on the strategy begins; consultative meetings are held in 27 areas of the departments of Cesár, Guajira and Magdalena.

1993   Formulation of the strategy becomes explicit, with all parties involved in the process.

1994   The new constitution opens up possibilities for sustainable development planning. A law is passed creating Corposierra. Asosierra is then set up at a departmental level, and the first local organization of leaders takes place at local level. Indigenous communities define the 'black line' or traditional territory. The national government recognises access to the sea for indigenous communities, thus guaranteeing their access to different ecosystems.

1995   The Presidential Office for the Atlantic Coast, the Ministry of the Environment, the National Planning Department, the Indigenous Affairs Division and the Pro-Sierra Nevada Foundation set up a joint working party for the formulation of a sustainable development plan for the Sierra Nevada.

Mata Atlántica, Brazil

Biosphere Reserve and Agro-ecological Exchange Network

Sebastião Salles de Sá, Governor of the State of Espíritu Santo and Edoardo Soares, APTA With the assistance of Luis Castello, IUCN

1 Introduction

The Mata Atlántica (Atlantic Forest Region) Biosphere Reserve programme in Brazil involves 14 federal states and federal government organizations, as well as the Association of Alternative Technology Programmes (APTA). APTA is a peasant exchange training network operating in six states: Río Grande do Sul, Santa Catarina, Paraná, Río de Janeiro, Espíritu Santo and Ceará.

In the state of Espíritu Santo – the case examined here – the biosphere reserve programme is coordinated by the State Department for Environmental Affairs (SEAMA). This department was set up to promote, in coordination with the private sector, public policies and actions aimed at facilitating sustainable development at the local level.

The Mata Atlántica biosphere reserve covers an area of 16,200 km², which is 36

MATA ATLÁNTICA, BRAZIL
Population:
Land area: 1,620,000 ha; plus agricultural zones
Ecological zones: Atlantic seasonal tropical forest
Main economic activities: agriculture, cattle, eucalyptus

per cent of the state. Espíritu Santo's biosphere reserve is considered a priority project in the state government's plans, and will act as an indicator and guide for the ecological and economic zoning scheme which is being prepared by SEAMA.

The Mata Atlántica Consortium, which is responsible for implementation of the strategy at the national level, is composed of the environmental departments of all the states (currently 14) taking part in the programme, and the Brazilian Institute of the Environment and Renewable Natural Resources (IBAMA), which is a federal body. The consortium will coordinate actions between the different states, find financial resources and foster exchanges of technical and scientific information.

The area suffers from severe structural and agricultural development problems resulting from the "green revolution" policies of previous decades, and from the cultivation of eucalyptus to produce cellulose. An association of agro-ecological producers was formed through field projects and technical exchanges to address these problems.

2 Objectives and Approach

The principal objective of the programme is to reverse the current deterioration of what is left of the Mata Atlántica; to improve the region's socio-economic conditions; and to raise the standard of living of the local population. The intention is to turn the Mata Atlántica into a biological corridor 4,000 km long.

These objectives are to be achieved through the following actions:

- consolidation of the state system of conservation units and scientific knowledge;
- passing of a forest policy law;
- forest supervision and monitoring;
- strengthening and promotion of environmental education projects;
- more demonstration units for sustainable development experiments; and
- establishment of a state management committee for the biosphere reserve.

The objectives of the APTA peasant exchange network are:

- to identify, develop and make available systems of production, processing and marketing developed by the farmers themselves;
- to organize a state agro-ecological exchange and mutual support network; and
- to promote agricultural production based on ecological sustainability through the provision of technical advice and assistance to farmers.

3 Relationship to Government Planning

In Espíritu Santo, the strategy is implemented by SEAMA, which is a state organization. At the federal level, SEAMA works closely with the National Environmental Programme (PNMA), which is the national coordination authority responsible for channelling funds to agencies from the World Bank. SEAMA also coordinates the work of other state departments that are responsible for different areas closely related to strategy implementation. These include the conservation units, of which 11 are under federal jurisdiction; 14 are dependent on SEAMA; 17 are under municipal jurisdiction and three are privately run. In addition, a planning department coordinates projects generated by the biosphere reserve.

4 Initial Development

The Mata Atlántica programme was set up in 1988 after the launch of the PNMA, which in turn is coordinated by IBAMA. The programme receives 75 per cent of its funding from the World Bank and 25 per cent from the federal government.

The programme started planning to preserve what was left of the Mata Atlántica on the Brazilian coast. Only some five per cent of the original subtropical forests remained, making the area one of the world's most threatened ecosystems, one in danger of complete extinction.

That same year, SEAMA was set up in the state of Espíritu Santo, with the conservation and recovery of this threatened ecosystem as one of its main institutional missions. A participatory planning process was initiated, involving federal and state institutions, NGOs, local inhabitants, municipalities, universities and specialists collaborating on a private basis.

At a very early stage, it was necessary to establish the area to be set aside for the biosphere reserve. This in turn required an official application to have the site recognized as part of the state's heritage (under the tombamento procedure). The request had to be made to the State Cultural Council, which is a government body consisting of representatives from 11 NGOs and two state governments. Discussions regarding the legal incorporation of the protected areas as part of the state heritage lasted until April 1991, at which time another procedure began to make the areas part of the biosphere reserve. This was achieved in November 1992. In this initial period, two main processes moved ahead simultaneously.

1. The Mata Atlántica Consortium began to negotiate with UNESCO's MAB to have the biosphere reserve approved. The Brazilian MAB Committee

(COBRA–MAB) was reactivated for this purpose. Originally the proposal covered the Mata Atlántica areas in the states of Río de Janeiro, São Paulo and Paraná. The following year, Espíritu Santo and Minas Gerais were added, followed a year later by Santa Catarina and Río Grande do Sul, and finally by the northeastern states. As a result, these areas came to be incorporated in the biosphere reserve and approved by UNESCO. Each of the successive incorporations gave rise to a different phase in the biosphere reserve procedure at the federal level.

2. Within the state of Espíritu Santo itself, there were a number of operational stages in the process. The initial preparatory stage consisted of marking out the areas, drafting the corresponding maps, preparing a technical document as the basis for the proposal, and holding the necessary working and discussion meetings among technical staff and representatives of the social sectors concerned with the strategy. The second or consolidation stage consisted of drawing up a register of projects required to implement the strategy. Altogether, 34 institutions participated in selecting 75 projects from the 323 proposed for the whole reserve. Some of these projects obtained funding and were able to start. Eventually the project register will be incorporated in an action plan, which was in the early drafting stage in 1993.

At the federal level, the biosphere reserve management system operates through a national council of 36 members, representing the federal government, state governments, universities and NGOs. In addition, there are regional technical boards which analyze technical and scientific issues; and state committees, which are in charge of administering resources, establishing priorities and approving action plans. The strategy also supports discussion forums, which are widely attended by local institutions, residents, and by NGOs working in related fields.

The SEAMA work team responsible for coordinating the strategy is composed of one coordinator, one lawyer to deal with legal matters, two biologists to plan conservation units and environmental education projects, three forestry engineers for the recovery of degraded areas and consolidation of conservation units, one civil engineer for forestry policy matters, one army representative for forest control, two administrators for administrative and financial matters and two students for support tasks.

The APTA Network

In the 1980s, as a result of the production crisis affecting the peasant community, the Brazilian Alternative Agriculture Meetings (EBAAs) were initiated. These biannual events brought together techni-

cians and students and a few farmers interested in developing a new technology base for agriculture.

At the second of these meetings (EBAA II, held in Petrópolis in the state of Río de Janeiro), a group of technicians agreed that, if agriculture was to move forward, a national inventory of all existing alternative agriculture experiments had to be drawn up. It was believed that a great deal of useful experience could be gleaned from small producers, who had actively opposed the advance of the "green revolution". The foundations were laid for the Alternative Technologies Project (PTA), which in just two years became established in five states: Río Grande do Sul, Santa Catarina, Paraná, Río de Janeiro and Ceará.

At this time, the officials in charge of some of the state departments of agriculture (in Paraná and Espíritu Santo in particular) expressed concern about the problem of peasants and the environment. In mid-1984, negotiations began between the PTA and the Espíritu Santo Department of Agriculture (SEAG) with a view to establishing a project in that state.

In September of that year, SEAG organized a state event on the theme of alternative technologies, which managed to bring together some 70 persons, mostly government technicians. One of the meeting's outcomes was the decision to conduct a

state inventory of alternative technology experiments. The Department of Agriculture assigned the task to the PTA, which began work in Espíritu Santo in December 1985.

One year later, another alternative technologies meeting was held in the state, this time with 150 participants, 132 of whom were farmers. To some extent, the meeting confirmed the ideas outlined in previous meetings regarding the need to develop alternative technologies for rural producers. From then on, the beneficiaries of the project took an increasingly active role, in a continuous effort to improve and extend the process.

An agreement with the government was finalized in 1987 and a PTA was set up for Espíritu Santo. It was a subsidiary of a Río de Janeiro NGO. In 1987, discussions began on converting the body into an autonomous NGO. This was accomplished in March 1990 with the foundation of APTA.

5 Implementation and Results

A general state system for environmental information is being created, whose principal aims are as follows:

- ecological and economic zoning (in the process of preparation);

- a coastal management project, under federal coordination; and
- a forest monitoring system.

Much is being done in the field of environmental education through pilot community projects. These include fishing schools for fishermen's children, who, in addition to subjects in the normal curriculum, are taught boat mechanics, ecology and methods of breeding marine species such as oysters. Similar schemes are run in rural schools. The valuable scientific and technical work performed by the Río Doce Forestry Commission has achieved recognition at national and international levels, especially in the field of woodland agriculture (agroforestry), management of native tree species, agroforestry systems (tropical agriculture under shade) and recovery of degraded areas using pioneer species in systems that simulate natural growth. These efforts are coordinated with those of APTA.

Another initiative has been the introduction of various types of forest gardens. These are model units used for the recovery of degraded areas, the enrichment of secondary forest, and so on. There is a plan to set up 29 of these gardens; nine were planted as of 1993.

Certain indicators have been defined to evaluate the effectiveness of the strategy in practice. In the case of the system of conservation units, for example, the following criteria were established:

- biodiversity conservation;
- increase in the population of endangered species;
- reduction in hunting;
- reduction in deforestation;
- increased research; and
- an increase in the numbers of visitors.

APTA's more notable results have included:

- improvement of state regulations through indirect pressure;
- better coordination between government and business forestry sectors and state conservation programmes;
- research and implementation programmes for the use of appropriate seeds and agro-ecological production techniques; and
- training of NGO technicians and students.

6 Lessons Learned

Several lessons have been learned during the process, including:

- the need to rely on the wholehearted support of policy-makers at the highest level and the need for the right institutions, such as SEAMA, to lead the strategy process;

- the need to bring other government sectors into the discussions and coordinate efforts with them, in order to form a consistent front when dealing with other parties (especially organizations responsible for credit policies, tax exemptions and other legal aspects which have to be consistent with the objectives of the strategy);
- the need for a multi-disciplinary team of specialists, with plenty of experience in dealing with complex processes such as strategies, and the ability to be flexible and share a common language and methodology with the other members of the team;
- when the strategy is implemented it becomes influenced and altered by day-to-day realities. Errors may occur either in the strategy or in planning and it is wrong to believe that a 'perfect strategy' can be achieved. There is no such thing, since reality always turns out to be more complex than expected;
- no method or strategy will work unless people believe in it. Strategists must be given practical responsibilities in implementing the strategy. Conversely, those who are active in the field should also be involved with planning. If they fail to understand the significance of their task in the context of the strategy as a whole, they will have difficulty developing any enthusiasm, which leads to inefficiency;
- the strategy's proposals must be viable – it is very important to test the attainability of goals. In the case of APTA, a great deal of importance was attached to short-term goals and actions. For example, within a short amount of time farmers were obtaining harvests without the use of agro-toxins or chemical fertilizers. This was modest proof that agro-ecology was possible; and
- the risk of error must not be allowed to prevent action. Sharing mistakes with others is a good way of helping to get things right, since one 'wrong' in practice is more instructive than 200 'rights' in theory.

7   Chronology

1983   Foundations are laid at the EBAA for PTA. In just two years the project is adopted in five states.

1984   PTA and the state of Espíritu Santo sign an agreement to undertake a state inventory of alternative technology experiments.

1986   Another Alternative Technology Meeting takes place in the state, this time attended by 150 participants, 132 of whom are farmers.

1988   The National Environmental Programme is started with World Bank funding and federal contributions. The Mata Atlántica Consortium is officially set up in 14 states, under the protection of the Brazilian Constitution, which declares the dry tropical forest of the Mata Atlántica as part of the national heritage. Creation of SEAMA for the state of Espíritu Santo.

1989   Approval of the technical document for the proposal, for submission to the World Bank, to create a biosphere reserve in the state. Start of procedure (tombamento) for recognizing areas of special ecological importance as part of the state heritage.

1990   Founding of APTA. The National Environmental Programme is given approval by the World Bank and spending on implementation activities begins.

1991   Tombamento procedure approved. Initial steps are taken to include areas of interest in the biosphere reserve and to seek UNESCO approval. The first instalment of the funding is received.

1992   UNESCO approves the incorporation of the demarcated areas in Espíritu Santo in the Mata Atlántica biosphere reserve.

1993   Discussions concerning the strategy action plan for the full implementation of the biosphere reserve.

Tambopata-Candamo, Peru

Eco-regional Strategy for Sustainable Development

THOMAS MOORE, EORI CENTRE
AVECITA CHICCHÓN, CONSERVATION INTERNA-
TIONAL WITH THE ASSISTANCE OF ALBERTO
SALAS, IUCN

1 Introduction

On January 29, 1990 the Reserve Zone of
Tambopata-Candamo (ZRTC) in the
Peruvian Amazon region was established
over an area of 1,478,942 hectares by
Ministerial decision. The decision was
obtained after years of lobbying by
conservationist groups for the protection
of the Tambopata River basin in the
departments of Madre de Dios (Inka
region) and Puno (Mariátegui region).
Initially the local inhabitants rejected the
establishment of a reserve zone because it
had been imposed upon them. This
attitude changed after some painstaking
groundwork efforts, undertaken chiefly by
the Eori Centre for Amazonian Research
and Promotion and by the coordinator of
the ZRTC on behalf of the Directorate of
Protected Natural Areas (formerly the
national parks programme).

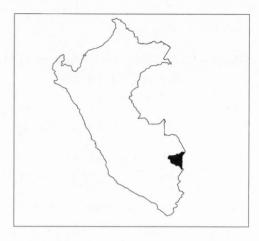

TAMBOPATA-CANDAMO, PERU
Population: 7,200; growing quickly
Land area: 1,478,942 ha
Ecological zones: Amazonian rainforest,
rivers
Main economic activities: timber, Brazil
nuts, alluvial gold, subsistence agriculture,
fishing, hunting

According to Peruvian law, a reserve zone is a provisional arrangement which should be replaced by an environmental planning order in accordance with the current and potential uses of its resources. The strategy described below is sponsored by the Directorate of Protected Natural Areas and Forest Fauna, which is itself part of INRENA. The directorate works through a technical team, which is in charge of designing the strategy. The team includes a forestry engineer, a regional planning specialist, an agricultural economist and a social anthropologist.

The strategy has generated a considerable amount of information, which has served as a basis for diagnoses and studies of the area. The Eori Centre, an NGO with its main office in Puerto Maldonado, has played a key role in the design and implementation of the strategy through its contacts with indigenous and farming organizations. The team has managed to obtain the combined support of the main indigenous organizations, settlers and NGOs. The technical and financial support of Conservation International (CI) has also been available throughout the process.

A series of production and marketing activities has begun among organizations in the area. These activities have mobilized grassroots organizations and, in the case of indigenous communities, have led to the recovery of part of their ancient territories.

This process of social mobilization has brought together grassroots organizations and NGOs engaged in social and conservation work under the umbrella of the Union for Sustainable Development of Madre de Dios (UDSMAD), coordinated by state conservation and development institutions. While the strategy has not yet been formalized as an official or consensus document, it does exist as a participatory process for sustainable development.

2   Objectives and Approach

The situation at present

The ZRTC is an area of Peru with considerable and unusual biological diversity. According to CI's Rapid Assessment Programme (RAP), no fewer than 200 species of trees have been found in less than one hectare, with a comparable degree of diversity among the fauna. Conservation of the territory, through protection and sustainable use, deserves to be a regional and national priority. The ZRTC is located in the departments of Madre de Dios and Puno. Some 3,200 inhabitants (as of 1993) live in the northern part of the zone (Madre de Dios), while the population of the southern area (Puno) amounts to some 4,000.

Despite its present low population density, this rich biodiversity is in danger of gradually disappearing unless measures are

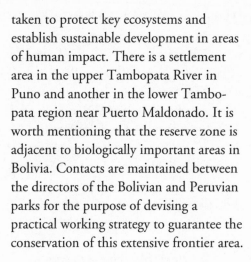

taken to protect key ecosystems and establish sustainable development in areas of human impact. There is a settlement area in the upper Tambopata River in Puno and another in the lower Tambopata region near Puerto Maldonado. It is worth mentioning that the reserve zone is adjacent to biologically important areas in Bolivia. Contacts are maintained between the directors of the Bolivian and Peruvian parks for the purpose of devising a practical working strategy to guarantee the conservation of this extensive frontier area.

Objectives

The general objective for the region is to consolidate conservation and sustainable development initiatives in the Reserve Zone of Tambopata Candamo and its area of influence. Specific objectives include the following:

- to introduce land-use planning for the ZRTC through zoning based on ecological, economic and social criteria;
- to identify, analyze and establish priorities between conservation and development alternatives in the areas of agriculture, stock-breeding, forestry, mining, tourism, water resources and the protection of ecosystems;
- to ensure the participation of the population and local organizations throughout the process, and strengthen their capacity for self-management and economic and social development;

- to propose alternative economic and financial means of guaranteeing sources of income for the population without a negative impact on the environment; and
- to analyze the situation and present capacity of existing organizations and institutions in order to implement recommendations arising from the strategy.

3 Relationship to Development Planning

The ZRTC's planning strategy is headed by the Directorate of Protected Natural Areas, making it part of an internal national plan for conservation. Owing to the current weakness of regional institutions in Peru, the strategy receives little support from regional bodies, but it has a greater level of support from the local authorities in Madre de Dios. In the ZRTC–Puno sector, the groundwork and lobbying at the local authority level has been rather weak because of the unfavourable political environment. In the Mariátegui region, proposals tend to be more geared to development, such as road building and settlement projects. It is hoped that the situation will improve under the management of new authorities, within the general framework of regional and national environmental management.

4 Initial Development

ZRTC was created in January 1990 after an initial period of lobbying. There was a negative reaction on the part of the people of Madre de Dios because the reserve zone had been imposed on them without any previous consultation. The first forum to discuss the future of the ZRTC was used to explain concepts, to request derogation from Article II of the decision establishing the ZRTC (which prevented the renewal of forestry contracts), and to generate support for planning among the population.

The Eori Centre carried out a census and completed other components of a general analysis in a joint effort with local communities and their federations, especially the indigenous Federación Nativa del Río Madre de Dios y Afluentes (FENAMAD) and the farmers' organization, Federación Agraria Departamental de Madre de Dios (FADEMAD). The Eori Centre also sought the support of the Association of Nut Growers and Agro-industrial Producers of Lago Valencia and the Association of Nut Producers and Tourist Services of Lago Sandoval.

This slow and painstaking work began by building up exhaustive documentation on existing legal rights over lands, timber, nuts, mining resources (alluvial ore), fishing, tourism and other natural resources and economic activities. When all the information had been collected, it was passed on to grassroots organizations and to the Ministries of Agriculture, Energy and Mines, Fisheries, Industry and Tourism, as well as local and regional planning bodies. None of them had ever had access to such a complete range of data.

A supporting technical team was set up under the Directorate for Protected Natural Areas to design a comprehensive conservation and development strategy. Consultation workshops on conservation and development topics were held with the four indigenous communities involved in the ZRTC. This led to the establishment of an Executive Committee, made up of the secretary for productive and extractive affairs of the Inka Region, his equivalent for the Mariátegui Region, and the Director of Protected Natural Areas.

A central element of this strategy has been its participatory character at every stage, including design, discussion, testing, implementation, modification, approval and evaluation. This degree of participation has been achieved by insisting on involving local populations in all decision-making, through municipal assemblies, federation congresses, workshops, the participatory implementation of activities and, above all, continuous and thorough communication with all the parties concerned.

5 Implementation and Results

The strategy has not been adopted in the form of an official consensus document. It does, however, exist in essence as a participatory process for sustainable development. This process has matured through joint actions in the field toward an objective shared by many sectors, and has been regularly reflected in new legislation or local planning agreements. In this sense, the results have been significant.

When the government established an Agricultural Development Fund in late 1991, representatives of the Inka regional government, with the support of the Eori Centre, asked FENAMAD and FADEMAD to define their priorities for agriculture development in Madre de Dios. This was the first time the local communities and their representative federations had been consulted regarding public investment in their region.

After much debate and consultation with grassroots organizations, FENAMAD's priorities were identified as territorial consolidation, confirmation of land tenure, extension and rectification of boundaries, and a request for communal reserves to protect forest wildlife. At the same time, FADEMAD requested support for soil recovery through agroforestry activities and for start-up capital to build processing plants for manioc and banana flour.

At the beginning of 1992, the two federations began implementing these activities with loans from the government and technical support from the Eori Centre. The activities have been very successful among the local communities, which have been keen to expand them to an extent which neither the Peruvian government nor the NGOs envisaged. An important feature of the strategy has been the alliance built up between FENAMAD and FADEMAD, a link between Amazonian indigenous peoples and settlers which is unusual in South America.

In January 1993, FADEMAD, supported by FENAMAD and backed by large numbers of local inhabitants, stormed the premises of Empresa Colonizadora del Arroz (ECASA), the former rice-farming enterprise. ECASA held a monopoly over the sale of rice until being abolished by the government at the end of 1992, at which time producers were left without protection but were also free to act for themselves. The two federations, supported by the Eori Centre, requested the support of the Ministry for Agriculture. Finally, on 5 February 1993, President Fujimori came to Puerto Maldonado with the Minister of Agriculture and handed over the premises of ECASA to the two federations for them to manage.

FENAMAD and FADEMAD then set up the Agro-industrial Production and Marketing Enterprise for the Province of

Tambopata (EPCA–Tambopata). This institution not only deals with the marketing of the rice harvest, as ECASA used to, but is also designing a strategy for the harvesting and marketing of a full range of varied crops. These include manioc, bananas, and, most particularly, permanent cultivation which can be combined with other activities of the programme for soil recovery. The main limitation on activities is now the lack of capital to take these plans a stage further. FENAMAD, with the technical support of the Eori Centre, is marking out boundaries and regulating the territory as fairly as possible, thus avoiding actual and potential boundary conflicts between settlers and indigenous communities.

Meanwhile, other NGOs have been promoting ecotourism and applied biology activities, which offer alternatives to traditional forest extraction in the ZRTC. Among the most interesting experiments are projects combining nature tourism with the production of nuts and fishing, in addition to subsistence agriculture. These activities are currently undertaken by the communities which make up FADEMAD, Lago Valencia (which is adjacent to the ZRTC) and Lago Sandoval (inside the reserve zone). Near the mineral banks of the Tambopata River, also inside the ZRTC, the NGO ECCO is running a macaw breeding project, which has been fairly successful and which offers commercial potential. Another interesting project

has been butterfly breeding in the Comunidad Nativa (Ese'eja group) Infierno, which is being run by the NGO CEB/TReeS.

The nut-growers were initially excluded by the general ban on extracting forest products within the zone. They have come together and, with the support of FADEMAD, FENAMAD and the Eori Centre, as well as all the institutions engaged in planning activities for the zone, have managed to overturn the ban. Nut-growing is now considered a sustainable economic activity and is therefore allowed in the ZRTC.

In 1991, an NGO called CANDELA PERU began a marketing programme aimed at providing more services for nut producers. The programme is now managing a significant part of the total output. Since 1993, CANDELA PERU has received funds from CI to extend its operational capacity, at a time when the government has done away with all existing subsidies for the export of non-traditional products and reduced the profitability of nut sales.

On the basis of these joint activities and the coordinated planning of sustainable economic alternatives, FENAMAD, FADEMAD, the Eori Centre, ECCO, TReeS, CANDELA PERU and the Asociación de Conservación de la Selva Sur (ACSS) joined forces in March 1993 to establish UDSMAD. This was set up mainly to allow joint financing of projects, so that all participants could have better access to financial sources in order to implement their conservation and sustainable development activities.

In addition, the Peruvian Foundation for Nature Conservation (FPCN), with ZRTC coordination, works on projects for the protection of the lower Madre de Dios River. These projects are carried out through the Santuario Nacional Pampas del Heath team. The FPCN has also joined with the Peruvian Society for Environmental Law (SPDA), the Conservation Data Centre (CDC) and the UDSMAD, setting up an advisory committee to assist the Directorate of Protected Natural Areas with its planning work in Tambopata.

Despite some conflicts between institutions, there is a will to cooperate, not only on the part of the local communities, but also by NGOs and government authorities, which previously had kept apart and had not thought in terms of participatory planning. In 1994, contacts were established between the directors of protected natural areas in Peru and Bolivia with a view to devising joint policies for the protection of the Tambopata-Heath and Madidi basins on the border between the two countries.

In 1993, a second forum was held to discuss proposals for land-use planning and sustainable development. Before the forum, both FADEMAD and FENAMAD spent a great deal of time with their communities explaining the scope and limitations of the proposals. The most important outcome was the approval of the land-use plan, which includes the creation of a new national park over an area of some 760,000 hectares. The proposed name for the park is Bahuaja, which is the name of the Tambopata River in the Ese'eja language.

6 Lessons Learned

The main limitations included:

- rivalries among NGOs, among public sector institutions and between the two factions. The struggle for scarce resources often gives rise to conflicts of authority, which hamper the strategy's progress;
- the opposition from some sawmill owners and other businessmen bent on short-term extraction of natural resources, as well as from ill-intentioned political authorities and other general troublemakers. A further complicating factor is the political uncertainty prevailing in Peru;

- the isolation and difficulty of access to the more remote areas, which while it has protected the resources of these areas from deforestation and the exploitation of natural resources, has also been an obstacle to communication between local populations; and
- the economic crisis which Peru is undergoing has had the effect of reducing sustainable development alternatives, bringing greater pressure to bear on natural resources in the area.

The main opportunities include:

- the previous experience of the Eori Centre in its efforts to organize and support local communities, a keynote of this being the personal willingness of team members to treat the indigenous inhabitants and poor farmers which make up the population of the ZRTC as equals;
- economic factors, such as the failure of the Banco Agrario's policies, which caused FADEMAD to oppose new sustainable development concepts and practices; and
- the worldwide trend towards environmental awareness, which encouraged a greater willingness in Peru and in the ZRTC to adopt the strategy.

The main lessons learned included:

- most importantly, that all serious, participatory planning takes time and patience if it is to succeed;
- differences between institutions have to be overcome and gains have to be consolidated, not only in the ZRTC, but in the whole of the Amazon region; and
- local inhabitants, through their representative organizations, must take on the process as their own. They themselves must develop contacts with the other organizations involved. The full participation of local inhabitants helps to ensure successful planning.

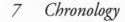

7   *Chronology*

1990   Creation of the ZRTC in January. The National Parks Directorate invites CI to support ZRTC planning. Preparation of the study "The State of Current Knowledge Concerning the Reserve Zone of Tambopata Candamo" by the Association for the Conservation of the Southern Forest and the Conservation Data Centre.

1991   First forum on the future of the ZRTC. The Eori Centre initiates a census and socio-economic study of the population of the Madre de Dios ZRTC and its area of influence. The NGO CANDELA PERU initiates a marketing programme for nut-growers. The government announces a fund for the development of agriculture in Madre de Dios, with the participation (for the very first time in this type of consultation) of FENAMAD and FADEMAD representatives, who define their priorities for the development of the sector.

1992   Rapid biological evaluation carried out by the CI's RAP in the Tambopata and Heath River basins. Socio-economic survey in ZRTC–Puno. Technical team selected to support National Parks Directorate for ZRTC planning.

1992   FENAMAD and FADEMAD successfully initiate activities, with loans provided by the government and Eori Centre technical assistance.

1993   In January, FADEMAD, with the support of the FENAMAD, storms the premises of the former rice-farming enterprise, ECASA. President Fujimori hands over the premises of ECASA to the two federations. CANDELA PERU receives CI funding to extend its operational capacity, at a time when the government eliminates subsidies for nut-growers. FENAMAD, FADEMAD, Eori Centre, ECCO, TreeS, CANDELA PERU and ACSS unite to found UDSMAD. Establishment of the government's executive committee for ZRTC planning. Completion of pre-feasibility study.

1993   Second forum to discuss the proposals for territorial planning and sustainable development. The most important conclusion gives approval for the land-use plan which includes the creation of a new national park.

Glossary

ACSS	Asociación de Conservación de la Selva Sur
ACTo	Tortuguero Conservation Area
AEK	Association of Kuna Employees
AHT	Agrar und Hydrotechnik
ANAP	National Small Farmers Association
APTA	Association of Alternative Technology Programmes
ASIREA	Loggers Association
Asosierra	Association of Sierra Nevada Municipalities
BMZ	Bundesministerium für Wirtschaftliche Zusammenarbeit
CANARI	Caribbean Natural Resources Institute
CATIE	Agroeconomic Research and Education Centre
CDC	Conservation Data Centre
CEBSE	Centre for the Conservation and Ecodevelopment of the Bay of Samaná and its Surroundings
CESP	Commission on Environmental Strategy and Planning
CI	Conservation International
COBRA	Brazilian MAB Committee
COMARNA	National Environmental Commission
CONAMA	National Environmental Commission
CONAP	National Council for Protected Areas
COPLASA	Planning Council for the Region of Samaná
CORPES	Regional Planning Council for the Atlantic Coast
DANIDA	Danish International Development Agency
EBAAs	Brazilian Alternative Agriculture Meetings
ECODES	National Strategy of Costa Rica

ECORAE	Institute for the Ecodevelopment of Amazonia		Nature Conservation
		GO	Governmental organization
ECOT-PAF	National Conservation Strategy for Sustainable Development and the Forest Action Plan for Nicaragua	IAF	Interamerican Foundation
		IBAMA	Brazilian Institute of the Environment and Renewable Natural Resources
EEC	European Economic Community	IDA	Institute for Agrarian Development
EIA	Environmental Impact Assessment		
		IDRC	International Development Research Centre
EPCA	Agro-industrial Production and Marketing Enterprise (for the Province of Tambopata)	IIED	International Institute for Environment and Development
FADEMAD	Federación Agraria Departamental de Madre de Dios	INRENARE	National Institute for Renewable Natural Resources
FAO	UN Food and Agriculture Organization	IPF	Physical Planning Institute
		IRENA	Institute for Natural Resources and the Environment
FAP	Forest Action Plan		
FENAMAD	Federación Nativa del Río Madre de Dios y Afluentes	ITTO	International Timber Trade Organization
FINNIDA	Finnish International Development Agency	IUCN	The World Conservation Union
FPCN	Peruvian Foundation for		
		IUCN-ORCA	IUCN Regional Office for Central America

JACASA	Council of Samaná Peasants' Associations	PAANIC	Environmental Action Plan (Nicaragua)
JAPDEVA	Ports and Atlantic Development Board of Administration	PACTo	Project for the Consolidation of the Tortuguero Conservation Area
KfW	Kreditanstalt für Wiederaufbau	PAFNIC	Forest Action Plan for Nicaragua
MAB	Man and Biosphere Programme (UNESCO)	PCODES	Conservation and Sustainable Development Programmes (Nicaragua)
MAG	Ministry for Agriculture and Stockbreeding	PDI-Petén	Integrated Development Plan (Petén)
MARENA	Ministry for Natural Resources	PDP	Prospective Development Proposal
MDR	Ministry for Rural Development	PEMASKY	Ecological Programme for the Management of the Forest Areas of Kuna-Yala
MIDEPLAN	Ministry of Planning		
MIRENEM	Ministry of Natural Resources, Energy and Mines	PNMA	National Environmental Programme of Brazil
NGO	Non-governmental organization	PNR	National Rehabilitation Plan
NORAD	Norwegian Agency for Development Cooperation	PNT	Tortuguero National Park
		PTA	Alternative Technologies Project
OLAFO	Conservation for Sustainable Development Project in Central America	RBC	Barra del Colorado Forest Wildlife Refuge

SEAG	Espíritu Santo Department of Agriculture		UNCED	UN Conference on Environment and Development
SEAMA	State Department for Environmental Affairs		UNDP	United Nations Development Programme
SEGEPLAN	General Planning Department (Petén)		UNEPET	Petén Implementation Unit
SIAPAZ	International System of Protected Areas for Peace		UNESCO	United Nations Educational, Scientific and Cultural Organization
SIDA	Swedish International Development Authority		UPAGRA	Small Producers' Association
SINAC	National System of Protected Areas		USDMAD	Union for Sustainable Development of Madre de Dios
SINADES	National Coordinating Body for Sustainable Development		WCS	World Conservation Strategy
SINAP	National System of Protected Areas		WRI	The World Resources Institute
SPDA	Peruvian Society for Environmental Law		WWF	Worldwide Fund for Nature
TFAP	Tropical Forest Action Plan		ZRTC	Reserve Zone of Tambopata-Candamo